mud BALL

Atulya K Bingham

"A joy from beginning to end – a brave, funny, moving account of building a new life and a new home out of mud in Turkey's mountain wilderness." **Sara Crowe, author of Bone Jack** (nominated for the Carnegie Medal in 2015).

"Throughout her book and the life she leads Bingham is an inspiration to us all. From start to finish her writing guides us through what for many of us is a metaphor for our lives: We have big plans, we stumble, and with perseverance and some good friends many times we succeed." **Chris Shaw, Turkey's first earthbag pioneer.**

"A work of gentle and progressive revelation, and great entertainment." **Philippa Rees, author of Involution.**

"I laughed out loud. The suspense had me sitting on the edge of my chair. Atulya K Bingham is a magnificent storyteller." **Sophie Hunter, strawbale builder of Dutoba.**

"Mud Ball provides rich fodder for the hungry dreams of would-be natural building enthusiasts. But its real value lies in its testimony of a journey towards freedom, and a life lived with joy." **Claire Raciborksa, author of Mariella.**

"A fantastic read, whether you are interested in natural building or not!" **Brigitte Muir OAM, the first Australian woman to climb Everest and author of The Wind in my Hair.**

Despite having very little money, almost no building experience, and endless naysayers who told her she would fail, Atulya K Bingham completed her lovely earthbag home. Her house has even survived three earthquakes. Her personal, inspirational story shows how anyone can build their own sustainable home with earthbags.

Dr Owen Geiger, Director of the Geiger Research Institute of Sustainable Building, author of *Earthbag Building*, and the two popular natural building blogs:

The Natural Building Blog (www.naturalbuildingblog.com)
Earthbag Building (www.earthbagbuilding.com)

mud BALL

Atulya K Bingham

The Mud

www.themudhome.com

MUD BALL

A MUDHOUSE BOOK

First edition published in the UK in 2015.

Back cover photograph by Melissa Maples.

ISBN 9781849147521

Reproduced, printed and bound in the UK by The MUD.

Acknowledgements

Sacks of gratitude are owed to the entire earthbag team. Writing this memoir has been almost as much fun as building the house.

I am indebted to the late Celal Aksoy for his dedication, for believing in my project, for his patience, his gorgeous stone work, and for lending me Apo the dog.

Adnan Khan went far beyond the call of duty. Among a host of other things, I'm deeply grateful to him for his immaculate screwing-in of my roof beams, for hot dinners on cold nights, for my kitchen wall, and for that unforgettable night when the rain threatened to destroy the floorboards.

Esra's strength and energy when whacking on the earthbags was a life-saver, not to mention her tackling of the barbed wire. Many thanks to her for her inspiring presence, conscientiousness, and for feeding me in the winter.

Gratitude is due Ahmet for sawing my entire floor by hand, for coming to find my phone with me in the middle of a hurricane, and for making me laugh when it all went wrong (which was often).

Many thanks to dear Dudu for planting my vegetable patch, for plying me with food when I was hungry, and most of all for respecting my privacy.

And of course much appreciation to Annika, for her sweat and toil at the outset. Also thanks to Elif Aysan for her ongoing support of the venture, and for cooking me dinner when I was too tired and hungry to cook my own.

Then there were those who helped from afar. As usual, I'm indebted to my dad for his tireless support, for lending me money when I ran out, for a plane ticket home in desperate times, and also for his valuable editorial comments.

Thanks to Chris Shaw, my uncle Nigel, and Pax Amphlett for sharing their building knowledge with me, and for their roofing ideas. Owen Geiger and Kelly Hart's *Natural Building Blog* was an indispensable resource, as well. I've no idea if my house would still be standing had it not been for *Earthbag Building, The Tools and Tricks of the Trade* by Kaki Hunter and Donald Kiffmeyer which was my earthbag bible.

Regarding the book itself, once again many thanks indeed to Claire Raciborska for her careful reading of the first draft, and her excellent feedback. Much appreciation to Helen Baggott for editing the manuscript. Thank you, as always, to Melissa Maples for the use of her photograph on the back cover, as well as the others that appear on *The MUD* website.

For Celal Aksoy, where ever he may be.

Author's Note

To the best of my knowledge, I've relayed the earthbag house adventure accurately, editing where necessary to maintain readability. Memory is a slippery creature, however. There may be things I have omitted or mistakes I have made, and of course, everyone remembers everything differently. For various reasons, the position of the ghost story was moved. Out of a respect for privacy, one or two identities were changed or made composite characters.

Table of Contents

The Beginning

'Kerry! I keep telling you, but you just won't listen. You need to build a house *now*! Winter is coming. A storm's coming. It says so on the telly.' My neighbour Dudu had appeared at my fence only the day before, wisps of hair darting out of her headscarf. 'And don't forget. You can always stay on my sofa...oh but you won't. I know!' She was wringing her hands. 'You're so stubborn. It's *English* stubbornness, that's what it is. God knows it'll be the death of you!' She huffed and puffed, popped her false teeth in and out, and shook her fist at me.

From the other side of the fence I looked down at her, not due to superciliousness but because she only reached my shoulder.

'I'll be fine, Dudu. The tent is raised off the ground now. Anyway I'm into storms, they're exciting.'

Dudu screwed up her eyes and turned away in disgust. But she wasn't the only one to fret over my houseless predicament. Celal, my wiry garden help, wandered up to the fence. He leaned on a large pickaxe and looked me up and down quizzically, his face a brown web of wrinkles.

'Aye, you wanna be building yourself a hut to park your bum in before winter, look at mine – didn't cost me a ha'penny but it does the job, eh?'

Celal always spoke using little or no punctuation and I was left squinting as I tried to work out what he said. Once the meaning dawned on me, I swallowed a reply. Well, I could see quite clearly his house hadn't cost a half-penny. It was something of a wonder that shack was still standing. My tent appeared by far the safer option.

'That weather's a comin' in, yer know and it's not all sunshine and cherries after that. Your arse'll be in the mud and you'll be swimmin' in it I tell yer, it'll be a swampahogshit that's what it'll be.

'A swamp of what?'

'Hogshit.'

I remembered that conversation now, and I slid deeper into my sleeping bag. Celal's warning echoed through the sleepless vale of my mind as I listened to sheets of rain break over my tent. I couldn't see it, but knew there was indeed a swampahogshit occurring on the other side of my canvas. As soon as I put a foot out of the tent, I'd step into it.

I'd known a deluge was on its way. My predicament was entirely of my own making. The wind had started its campaign up the slopes in early evening. I'd watched the invisible wheel of air roll through the forests. It parted the bushes like hair. My tent was perched on a wooden platform I'd hammered together a month before. As the light faded and the wind began lowing ominously, I had run around the legs of the platform with pieces of thick rope in my hands. One by one, I tied the corners of the tent to the platform

15

legs. It was a mess of knots a sailor would have cursed at. I placed four large rocks into each corner of the tent for good measure. My lamp and laptop were charged. As darkness fell and I peered inside, I felt a wave of satisfaction. It was a canvas bubble. Everything looked hunky-dory. The wild outside was where it should be (out) and my cosy familiars were in their rightful place (in).

But that had been four hours ago. Now, the sky was as black as Pluto's subconscious. High winds were bending fifty-year-old pine trees like saplings, and rain wasn't falling. It was flying. It was a water-breathing dragon, a dragon that had taken a peculiar dislike to my tent door and was throwing torrents at it as though it needed extinguishing. Credit where credit is due. My fifty-dollar tent from Carrefour was doing its level best. It was a canvas St George, ducking and bending in the face of the crazed beast above. I have bought a number of cheap tents from supermarkets since then, always hoping for the same level of durability. I have been continually disappointed.

Soon, I began to think I was swimming. The awning buckled under the storm, and I felt something wet on my cheek. The side of the tent had flattened under a gust. Then, to my consternation, the top half of my body rose into the air. I realised the rear of the tent had lifted clean off the platform with nothing but the tethers yanking it back down. I remembered a tale (perhaps tall) I'd heard of a hapless camper whose tent had been blown from a cliff-face with him still in it. The tent had sailed down like a parachute. I couldn't recall, as I pulled my sleeping bag up to my chin, what condition the poor fellow had reached the ground in.

It might seem odd, but in a strange sort of a way, I was happy. There was still a fiction in my mind that I was inside (safe) and trouble was outside. And then it happened. The tent membrane gave up. It changed from a separator of worlds into a flimsy strip of permeable tarp, into a point of exchange.

Points of exchange are powerful. They are precious. They are nodes of creation. Building a house of mud was never a dream of mine. The idea sprouted quite suddenly in response to the land and the seasons. It grew out of the point of exchange between me and my environment. If this adventure is about anything at all, it's about that sacred line of connection where the Known meets the Unknown. Because it's there that magic happens. It's there you find the strength and the courage to build real dreams. Books, videos, training manuals, courses and teachers are just dry seeds, atomised particles floating about the air of your mind. It's not until the theory touches the earth, and the earth touches the theory that anything beautiful manifests.

The outside invaded quite subtly considering there was a hurricane going on. I felt one cool drop on my forehead and then another on my chin. Nothing dramatic. Just a little wet. I smiled. It was still fine. I'd probably make it until dawn. Reaching up, I flicked on my solar lamp. Everything was bathed in an eerie blue glow as the lantern, now swinging, cast a ring of pale light above and around. The ring bobbed from left to right like a celestial pendulum.

It was then I noticed small pools of water collecting in the corners of the tent. Teasing my belongings from the edges, I came to terms with the fact I probably wouldn't sleep that night. I maintained a vigilant eye on the tent corners, as if by staring at them, they'd buckle up and become watertight. They didn't. The pools spread. My hair was now seaweed damp. The bottom of my sleeping bag had developed a dark, wet splodge. It spread like black, comfort-munching fungus. *Shit! My laptop! My books!* Gathering everything I valued into the centre of the tent, I huddled over this loot in the foetal position. The rain kept sliding in.

All campers are familiar with this feeling, in particular those resilient wellie-wearing troupers from the British Isles. Such nights are miserable, sleepless swamps. At least in the UK one can usually expect to be able to run for cover. To sleep in the car. Find a hostel. The storms of the Mediterranean in winter are ruthless. I could clearly hear tree branches cracking apart in the forest next door. How had I forgotten what winter was like until this moment? How could I *ever* have conceived the idea of bedding down outdoors through December, January and February? The only reason my tent was still on the platform was the tethers and the weight of everything inside it (a suitcase of books makes great tent ballast). Slowly but surely, terror wormed its way into me. The outside was no longer out. The inside was no longer safe. Anything could happen. I was at the mercy of the gods. At any given moment the canvas could be ripped asunder, and it would be over.

I did have a car I potentially could have slept in, but I honestly wasn't sure how to reach it. The same applied for Dudu's house. Finding her door half a kilometre away would have been an outright gauntlet of gulches-turned-rivers, flying branches and hefty gusts. If by some miracle I did arrive at her porch in one piece, I was going to be sodden from head to toe without as much as a change of undies. The dormouse in me reasoned hibernation was the best strategy.

Thus I huddled there. Every now and again, the canvas would flatten onto my face and soak me. The pools in the corners joined forces to become a moat of dirty water. It rippled about a dwindling island upon which was stranded a laptop, a small suitcase and a human. I admit it; I prayed. I prayed to the land. I prayed to the sky. I prayed to the more resilient, sensible parts of myself. I prayed to my inner guides. I prayed to the universe. 'I just want to make it till morning,' I whined.

Then a miracle happened. A warble slid through the churning, huffing night. I recognised it as my saviour. The call to prayer. That morning, it was Ali hoca in the valley below who was the first to arrive at his post, which was a surprise, as he was notorious for oversleeping. I often wondered at the muezzins in weather like this. How had he possibly managed to reach the mosque? Never have I been happier to hear his voice. The call to prayer held practical significance. Although the sky now appeared as deep and lightless as a dungeon, dawn was imminent.

As Ali hoca crooned, he was followed in the round by the indefatigable muezzin of Brook neighbourhood – a half-hamlet comprising half a dozen charming stone houses occupied by artists from Istanbul, hippies and mountaineers. The two voices mingled and danced through the ruckus outside. They had almost finished when, last but not least, the loudspeaker of the village mosque rattled and coughed to life. The village muezzin, no doubt sleepless and with half a mind on his polytunnel of tomatoes, banged out a call to prayer in minutes.

Then it fell silent. Without warning, the wind fell away. The rain thinned to a patter. The sky lightened. The storm gurgled, writhed on the horizon for fifteen minutes, and died.

As my dank canvas world brightened, I tentatively sat up. I rubbed my eyes, flattened my hair back and picked my way gingerly out of the mess of my sleeping bag. Grimacing at the pond that had collected at the front of the tent, I unzipped the front door. I squinted. Then I crawled out, and fell slap bang into a swampahogshit.

The Foundations - Part One

Is there ever a beginning, a ground zero from which we start out fresh, unhampered by the ordeals of that which went before? Day by day we are constructing the house of our lives, each word, gesture and experience becoming another brick in the edifice. Then there is that which lies below the surface. The foundations. Our memories are the footings that our futures are built upon. They create us.

***

I had always been a teacher. First, I was a modern languages teacher in a secondary school in the UK. I was in my early twenties and would catch the Tube to Barnet every day to wage a war of education with classes stuffed full of disinterested adolescent males (it was a boys school). I'd write the date on the white board in French (*jeudi dix décembre*) and flinch as they'd chorus 'Judy dicks December' in return.

Then in the mid-nineties, I moved to Turkey. I found a job in an international school with a total of ten children who could all pronounce the date perfectly in at least four languages. I soon left there to become an independent English teacher for adults. I spent many happy hours discussing Marx, Freud, Fellini films and Milan Kundera with university lecturers. Eventually, I became a yoga teacher, too.

Economically speaking, teaching was a large, plush cushion I could collapse in whenever the need arose. Whatever happened, wherever I went, I knew I could earn a living. Sometimes I earned more than a living because tutoring English in Turkey in the early noughties was lucrative. I worked three days a week and still managed to buy a beautiful plot of land and a brand new Toyota Yaris. I never worried about money. Education was an enormous, lira-bristling money tree. And then I did something foolhardy. I sold my car, borrowed some money and opened a yoga centre with a partner a few hundred kilometres along the south coast. It had been a dream I'd cherished for ten years. Within six months I was bankrupt.

The saga of The Yoga Camp deserves its own tome, but this is not the time. In short, I established a low impact backpacker camp with my partner, who for the sake of anonymity I shall call Volkan, in an unspoilt enclave near Fethiye. We started the project in February 2009, throughout March we both worked ourselves into the ground to open it, we were inundated with guests by April (despite not actually having finished the construction of the thing), fought numerous battles with the police, the forestry commission, corrupt health and safety officials and equally fraudulent planning authorities, by May we loathed each other, by June my partner was to be found knocking back beer at ten am, playing loud techno music and getting stoned at the bar, while I took up chain smoking and experienced something of a breakdown. A war of attrition began, the viciousness of which is rarely encountered outside a partnership collapse. In July I ran away and left Volkan to it. By September he was no longer paying back my initial investment. I managed to claw a large portion of it back by plumbing my psychic depths and pulling out a character not wholly dissimilar to Bellatrix Lestrange. Even so, by October I was more or less bankrupt. The only asset I had left that wasn't collateral for my debts was my land. I'd gone from high-flyer to pauper in six months.

The last day in The Yoga Camp will probably remain engraved in my memory for many years. I was sitting on a bench watching Volkan and a troupe of workers construct a new two-storey wooden platform known locally as a köşk. It's something like a simple gazebo. The pines that gripped the sharp slopes about the valley were whispering down to the sea. The small, white bay held the Mediterranean like a rocky glass of petroleum. I bit my lip. It felt as though my innards were being peeled away from my skin. My dream had failed. I had failed.

I watched the men dig holes for the support poles of the platform, and scribbled a few diagrams in a notebook. It was a practicality. I loved nature, and wanted to live close to it. But now, I thirsted to be independent, to survive in the wilds without needing someone else. I reasoned if I could just learn how to put a platform together, I could camp on it.

25

Velcroing my eyeballs to the guys, I searched for clues into the nebulous art of hammering.

Volkan sauntered over. He was gripping a can of beer in one hand and toying with a hand-rolled cigarette in the other. He peered over my shoulder at my amateur sketch. 'What are you doing?'

'Just making a few notes.' I shrugged.

'You'll *never* be able to do this,' he said, and wandered back to the platform. The other four young henchmen he was presiding over stopped to look at me for a moment. Or look me over. One or two laughed. The others smirked. Then they carried on with their duties of post-propping while the ample-bellied carpenter measured up the platform.

'You'll *never* be able to do this.'

At the time I was mortified. I think I might have even sobbed, albeit quietly while no-one was looking. But as time goes by, I see this situation is more universal than at first appears. Who doesn't have self-doubt heckling from their psychological stalls and keeping them in their place? The reason put-downs like this have power, is because deep down we believe them.

You want to live off-grid in a house you built with your own two hands? You want freedom from the grind? You want clean food, clean air and independence from the system? I say, if you want it and you haven't yet created it, it's because there's a 'You'll *never* be able to do this', in your head sabotaging your mission. The question is, what are you going to do about it?

Ironically, three years later when I moved onto my mountain with not much more than a tent, it was those selfsame words that saved me. Over time they became my mantra. A small-minded opinion to take hold of, twist and stamp out of existence.

'You'll *never* be able to do this.'

'*Oh really? I'll do what you're doing, and I'll times it by ten, arsehole!*'

Never let it be said that I've taken an insult lying down.

The Foundations – Part Two

Let's return to a bedraggled tent perched on a platform high up on a lonesome hill, to the morning after that fateful storm in late October 2011.

The Mediterranean's weather is a strange beast. Storms well up out of nowhere. A few boisterous gusts and a darkening horizon are the only hints of the madness to come. Then a knife of lightning rips the sky in two letting a roof-shaking mortar attack of thunder through. But just as quickly the hurricane vanishes. A new day arrives. All is still. The sun bursts apart the morning. Flowers open with a confidence that is quite arresting. The birds are twittering, and everything is wonderfully bucolic.

An hour after I'd crawled out of my soggy canvas bubble, I was greeted by a golden morning of fresh smelling earth and glittering pine trees. My tent was standing stalwart on its platform; a canvas survivor if ever there was one. My car wasn't quite as fortunate, or hardy. At that time, I owned a rough and ready, second-hand Turkish Fiat, a model known as a *Sahin* which translated as Buzzard in English. In fact Fiat had misnamed it. Flight and chase were as far from the *Sahin's* repertoire as space travel or submarine adventure. It was a slow, no nonsense machine designed to cope with the pot-holed strife of rural Turkish roads. Donkey would have been far more appropriate name for this lurching, snorting beast of burden. On any other day it could handle my asphalt-less 30% gradient track as efficiently as a jeep. The trouble was, I no longer had a track to speak of. I had a swampahogshit instead.

I was just considering this when Celal climbed over Dudu's fence and onto my land. He was wearing a pair of wellington boots and a cap pulled jauntily down over one ear. His dog Apo was on his heel. Apo was an enormous Anatolian shepherd that almost reached Celal's waist. In fact, in circumference, Apo was probably the larger. With his thick, grey-tipped fur and his massive black head, he was intimidating to those who didn't know him. To those who did, he was their guardian. I loved Apo. He had spent all summer watching over my land as I camped on my hill. He would amble over at nightfall and curl up outside my tent. I'd relish the sound of his heavy breathing the other side of my canvas wall and feel unassailable.

As Celal approached my besieged tent, Apo trotted gamely behind him cocking his leg over the compost heap, and then the tent-platform post.

'Aye, just came to sees you were alright an' all that. We need to cover that tent up with plastic, that'll stop it leakin'. Ah, we're gonna be mudwrestling in a ringacrap for the next few days, that we are.'

I pushed a smile from my face. It was as weak and uninspiring as Starbucks coffee.

'Celal, I need a house.'

30

'Well course yer do! We've bin telling you that from the beginning. You've left it a bit late though eh? S'nearly winter!'

'I'm worried about the car. How will I get it out?'

My car was, at that point, a vessel of survival. I used it to bring water onto my aqua-starved land. Despite the sogginess, I was going to run out of clean water by evening, which meant my already basic standards of hygiene would slip into the territory of the squalid.

Celal wrinkled up his nose and adjusted his cap. 'Aye, roads a right shitfest.'

We both walked up to the car to assess the situation. We looked up and down the slope and tested the spongy, wet surface with our booted feet.

'You'll have to floor it. Nowt else you can do unless you're planning on staying 'ere forever. I'll get out and push if you get stuck.' My trusty Celal was looking as though he was already regretting having popped over.

The pair of us climbed in the donkey-buzzard and yanked the doors to. I started her up. And she did start, which was something of a miracle as she was LPG powered and none too keen on cold, damp mornings. I edged her round, pointed her in the direction of the slope, muttered a quick prayer and 'floored it'. We got up a nice speed on the first 100 metres to the base of the slope, though the engine was howling a little. Then came the incline. It was like trying to drive up an oiled skateboard rink. The wheels skidded. The car slid left and right. I wrestled with the steering wheel and roared quite a few profanities to which Celal nodded in approval. We careered on up and nearly made it until the mud simply became too deep and the incline too sharp. The wheels span, kicking mud behind us. We ground to a spluttering halt. Celal sighed and opened the door.

There are angels everywhere, which is a stroke of luck if you're a maverick like me. Yet we are all blessed with them. Ever felt the spontaneous desire to go out of your way to assist someone for no obvious personal gain? For that instant, the angel in you has been called upon. There is no doubt in my mind, Celal *was* my angel – a small, skinny, sun-wrinkled angel whose trousers were always too big. This was just one of many times he would be there to save me.

Accepting his lot, he made his way to the back of the car and rested his hands on the boot. I restarted the engine and pressed the gas. The wheels span. I tried to rock the car forwards and back to ram the mud a bit flatter (futile on a steep hill as I only slid backwards). I accelerated slowly. I revved quickly. It was no good. Celal was shin-deep in mud and my car looked like it had been defecated on from a great height, which metaphorically speaking it had. I banged my head on the wheel and groaned.

'Oh what am I going to do now?'

Celal waded round to the front window, looking fairly well excreted upon himself.

'Aye. We'll have to get the tractor to get us out now, you'll have to call Kemal.'

I sat bolt upright at that.

'Kemal? *Kemal*? You mean that arrogant boar I turfed off my land the other day? He'll never come. He *hates* me!'

It couldn't have been more than five days prior that I had engaged in a face-off with Kemal. Unbeknown to me he was the second in command to the village chief. I'm not the most sociable person in the morning, and I hate unexpected visitors. Suffice to say when Kemal's four-wheel drive had rolled down my slope to park above my land at nine am, I was far from hospitable. I hadn't let him cross the boundary. In the end he left in a huff, shaking his fist and yelling, 'You don't know who I am! *You'll* be sorry!'

Now I realised only too well who he was. He was The Man With The Tractor, and I *was* sorry.

'Well there's nowt else to be done, he's the only one with a tractor round these parts, pah! I'll talk him round,' Celal said. He fumbled in his pocket and pulled out his phone.

Somehow Celal persuaded the recalcitrant Kemal. After a lengthy confab it was agreed that 20 lira would pull the Buzzard up the hill. Celal squinted at the dashboard of his phone, before sliding it into his pocket. Then he turned to me and grinned, his moustache bristling silver in the sun.

Within ten minutes the tractor was roaring toward us. Chains were lashed around the massive wheels of what looked like a motorised, red elephant. Kemal was perched on the top. He refused to look at me, sticking his head in the air with a surly pout. I couldn't help but notice his eyes were crimson from a pot binge. Taciturn, he reversed his tractor the length of my slope. Then he hopped down into the mud, and angrily chained my car to his tow bar. I slid into the driver's seat of my Buzzard to steer where necessary. The tractor pulled away. It churned the mud beneath its killer tyres. Then it skidded, my bonnet swinging precariously on the chain behind it. For a moment I thought we wouldn't make it. But finally, our noisy convoy lurched forwards, and we slid upwards to the 'main' road.

***

I ruminated on all that mud over the next two days while my land was drying out; the slipping and sliding, the arbitrary subsidence. I had already noticed in the four years since I'd bought the property, how the earth slid every year from top to bottom. The land under our feet may appear solid and fixed, but in truth it is anything but. It moves with the seasons, with the weather and with earthquakes, of which there are many in Turkey. Even so, despite the obvious shifting sands of reality, we humans nonetheless delude

34

ourselves stability is attainable, that there is a solid point that we can tether our lives to, a rock of truth we can throw our emotional anchors under. We hope if we can just plan well enough, lay firm enough foundations, or dig deep enough, that we'll survive the winds of change. It's nonsense. We won't. One day the house of our life collapses and we have to move on regardless.

It is in the name of this unending quest for stability most people who build houses draw up plans. That's what architects are for, after all. They outline what the house will look like, how many rooms, how much it will cost and how long it will take. They compose neat lists of materials and sketch maps of their plot. They trace where electricity wires and water pipes will be laid, how large the windows will be, which part of the construction will be undertaken when.

I'm not quite sure to what extent living in Turkey – a country where future planning doesn't get you very far – has contributed to my aversion, but I simply can't be bothered to plan. I mean what's the point? Nothing ever goes to plan, does it? Has anyone in the entire history of human civilisation ever experienced life obediently following a schedule? I haven't. Is it that I've been singularly struck by bouts of plan-failure? Or is it that plans, being games we play in our minds, simply aren't grounded in reality?

Anyway, unlike the vast majority of house designers, I had no plan. No sketch. Nothing but the vaguest concepts of the kind of house I was going to build. The only clear aspect of the building in my head was that it was to be devoid of corners. I wanted curves everywhere, soft flowing circles. A round house.

The next day I sat at my wooden table perched in the mud on my one completed terrace. A fresh pot of coffee stood in the centre, and as I poured myself a cup, I inhaled the view of the mountains. They rose and fell about the land in bristling green layers that rippled down to the sea. The morning sun had turned the pines chartreuse. It was enchanting. Inspiring. My laptop was on the table, screen flipped up. I sighed and turned my focus back on the gadget. Having no power meant that I enjoyed a maximum of two hours' battery life before I'd have to drive somewhere to recharge. I grabbed the mouse, clicked and watched the screen turn Google white.

Back near Fethiye, Chris Shaw, an American friend of mine, had recently completed a series of earthbag roundhouses. It was the first time someone had tried the technique in Turkey. A month ago, I had visited him. I'd adored the Smurfish toadstool bungalows, the lumpy walls, the cave-like interiors. He had said it was a simple process, and my land comprised plenty of earth. All I needed were the sacks and some help. Bolstered by one of the many manic flashes of unsubstantiated positivism I am famous for, I typed 'how to build an earthbag house' into the box on the screen and hit enter. It mattered little to me that six months prior I hadn't even known how to bang a nail in. Nor that no one in Turkey knew what an earthbag house was at the time. I just liked the look of the thing.

'Aye, what we doing today, then?'

The next day Celal was back. He walked briskly up to the stick I'd banged into the ground, dubiously eyeing the three metres of washing-line string attached.

'Erm, building a house.'

Celal nodded perfunctorily as though I'd told him we were planting a row of potatoes rather than about to embark on a major construction project of which neither of us had the slightest clue what we were doing.

'What kind of house? I hope it's something wooden because I know how to do that.'

I grimaced.

'Actually it's something called an earthbag house. It's going to be round and made of bags of mud. Only one other person has tried this in Turkey.'

Celal squinted at me and pulled his cap down. He turned and walked silently to the tool shed. After a few moments, he came out with a shovel and a pick.

'Earthbag. Never heard of it. Dunno much about round either. Tell me where to dig and I'll dig, but all I can say is, I hope it doesn't take much more than a month, because that weather's comin' in, and when it does you'll be needing a roof over yer head.'

I drew a nice neat circle by turning the three metres of washing line round the stick. Celal murmured in assent. Then he raised the pick and began taking chunks out of the earth. Within an hour it became clear, if I didn't climb in that circle and dig, we weren't going to finish it. So I grabbed the pick, he took the spade and round we hacked like a pair of grunting, stone-mining goblins.

Foundations are arguably the most important part of the building process. They are what the entire structure of your house is resting upon. Once foundations are laid and constructed upon, they can't be altered. In hindsight, I see these foundations are not simply the channels you dig under your house. At that early stage of the building process, I wasn't aware how important other types of foundations were going to be. The psychological ones. The social ones. The team-leading ones. My hitherto life experiences had dug a good deep trench in my soul, which was just as well. It was all fine and dandy to crawl out of the mud after the storm, call Celal and flippantly inform him we'd start building a house in two days. But I was wholly inexperienced. I had no power or running water on the land.

Money was in short supply. Winter was but a month away. Any sane builder worth half his or her weight in Black and Decker hand tools, would flinch at the challenge of completing a house in a month. Luckily, I wasn't a builder at the time. I was blissfully ignorant of pretty much everything that lurked ahead.

***

That evening, once Celal had left, I stared at the ring of freshly dug earth. My shoulders were throbbing plaintively, and my arms were so tired I could hardly lift the teapot. The sun had dipped behind the outline of the mountains scraping a strip of burnt sienna out of the sky. My guts twisted. The foundation circle looked like an alien imprint, a developmental imposter in my wilderness. Everything was changing. The Unknown was cantering toward me at speed, but it was a masked rider and I couldn't see whether it was smiling at me or leering.

I switched my gaze to my tent. The canvas rippled under the touch of a light breeze. It was a picture of impermanence. Tents destroy almost nothing upon their erection, and barely leave a mark when dissembled. Stumbling slightly, I made my way to the wooden platform. I perched on its edge and smelled the canvas, nostalgically recalling the summer. I remembered what had prompted me to become a hobo scrabbling for existence up here in the first place...

Back in 2009, directly after the failed yoga camp incident, I needed money, and fast. Thus, I slumped back onto my trusty, economic beanbag of teaching. Only I chose to leave Turkey to do it. Instead, I tried something new and migrated to Taiwan. I spent a year and a half there, grafting in a Taiwanese primary school. It was my first encounter with The System in years, and the experience made a deep impression on me; rush hour traffic, bolted breakfasts, punch-in clocks, wage slips, staff meetings, clock-watching, the lurching dread on a Sunday night, the killing of time until Friday. Despite having worked freelance for most of my adult life, the security of a monthly salary soon drew a noose of convenience about me. By 2011 I'd almost pushed my financial head above water, nonetheless I felt a surge of anxiety about leaving. This is what it means to be a wage slave. One sinks into a bed of dull comfort, unaware the sheets are soaked in chloroform.

Yet I did leave. I was about to touch 40, and had an unfinished dream to realise. Thus, I flew back to Turkey, back to the Mediterranean, to the area where my land was. Two South African friends from Taiwan joined me. It may seem hard to believe after the previous yogic fiasco, but the plan was for us to create another spiritual camp, this time on my land.

Some people never learn.

***

'Spirit Circle?'

'Nah, too airy-fairy. We need something that represents the Earth too.'

'Hmm, think of round buildings.'

'Igloo, lighthouse, temple?'

'Temple? Urgh, sounds heavy and religious.'

'What about a yurt? That's a round building.'

'Yurt? Ya, that's both sustainable and friendly. Now we need an adjective, something spiritual.'

'Hmm, spiritual? Mystical? Ha! *Mystic* Yurt.'

'Mystic Yurt? Ya, I like that!'

'Me too. Mystic Yurt... Yes, excellent. That really sums it up.'

The three of us clinked our tiny Taiwanese tea cups, and drank to our future.

Spring was late coming that year. The Turkish Mediterranean remained a ruckus of grey unrest. Cool winds whipped over the mountains pushing sodden clouds through the valleys. People snuggled up in their homes with blankets on. I stayed with my South African friends in a seaside village about 15 kilometres from my land. We planned and talked and projected about our Mystic Yurt.

But something wasn't right. All three of us were exhausted from our battle with the education machine. Now that we had escaped its clutches, the world looked more open and bubbled with choices.

Within weeks, we backed out from our project. My chums returned to South Africa to start a foundry and a small farm. I was left in Turkey, relieved but lost. A midlife crisis loomed. Somehow I had to restart my life, only it felt like my battery was flat, the spark plugs needed changing and someone had tampered with the steering.

'Come and teach us English again,' came the cries from the city. 'Come and lead yoga groups again,' came the pleas from the valley. I buckled up and prepared myself for another dash on the teaching wheel.

It was then at this most inappropriate of times, in a place that was far from financially stable, I woke up one day and realised I couldn't teach another lesson. I simply didn't have it in me. Perhaps it was burn out. Perhaps it was simply time. I don't know. All I know is I just couldn't muster the drive. I had just purchased my donkey-buzzard and had little more than $6000 left in the bank. My abundant money tree had withered and died. God only knew what I'd do next.

This is how I found myself moving onto my virgin plot of land with not much more than a tent. I hadn't ever camped alone until that point, and certainly not somewhere without running water or power. But I needed a shelter, a space of my own, somewhere I could regroup and think. My land was the only place I could live without rent, thus enabling me to stretch out my resources a while. I had no idea what I'd do when the money ran out. I abandoned my fate to the gods and to my land. My land appeared to be the one that listened.

All through the summer I remained up there, shunning guests and communing with the dirt. Those six months scrabbling about in the earth affected me profoundly. They transformed me. I began to experience how little we need to feel complete, how the natural world heals us, and how this ball of mud we call planet Earth is our home. Our family. Where we came from. The nights were star speckled velvet duvets under which I slept like the child of the moon. The dawn was an ecstatic explosion of colour and birdsong. Evenings were dusky calls to a spirit world I'd forgotten existed. Something primal awoke in me, and with it I accessed a creative drive that was startling.

I began to build small and basic structures from bits of wood lying around. Initially, I did this out of sheer necessity, because I didn't have the money to pay a carpenter. From the very first day, it dawned on me how, despite plenty of meditation and yoga retreats, there were parts of me that had never seen the light of day. To think, all those years I'd had no inkling I loved building things.

Building wasn't just something I undertook because I had to (like cooking God help me). It was a passion. The feeling of creating something, *anything*, from the resources around is simply so fulfilling. Out of the dust of the old, a new life was born. And it looked nothing like it had before.

'Ah that's my girl! You're away now, look at *that*, isn't it lovely!' said Dudu, shouting over the fence. It was September now. I'd been camping on my land for nearly five months.

'Celal, I didn't know you still had it in you, eh?' Dudu guffawed and sent a few sparrows twittering into the air behind her. She might have only been five feet tall, but she still zipped over the metal boundary in one swift steeple-chase worthy leap. Hitching up her *şalvars*, my little, old neighbour walked to the shed Celal and I had just put together. She slapped the wooden walls, opened the door, walked in and out, and closed it again. 'Ooh all you've got to do now is nail in a few shelves and you'll be away, nice as pie. Then you can just make a bigger shed, like Celal's, and that can be your house. You'll need a roof over your head soon, Kerry, September's here, you know.'

'I don't want a house, Dudu. I love living in my tent.' I sighed. We had this conversation at least once a week and it pained me.

Dudu pulled her lilac flowered headscarf out of her eyes, tucked her hair in and scowled. 'Bah! You'll be sorry. *You'll* be sorry. You don't know what it's like in winter. You'll catch your death of cold. It'll be raining in buckets, flooding even! Mud everywhere!'

'Aye, we'll all be mudwrestling in a ringacrap,' added Celal definitively. Apo, who was slumped in a furry heap by Celal's feet, raised a doggy eyebrow and exhaled.

Materials

The materials required for an earthbag house are few and far between, and this was fortunate because driving to my land was something of an endeavour, particularly with cargo. All I bought at the outset was 1000 polypropylene sacks sewed to size, 20 sacks of hydraulic lime, barbed wire and gravel. The sacks had already arrived and were sitting under a blanket next to the shed, to protect them from the sun. Polypropylene holds firm in the damp, but inflict sunlight upon it and it soon disintegrates.

'Lime? What kinda lime? Whatcha gonna do with it?'

I was sitting in a hardware store about half an hour drive from my land. The township was an agricultural blot on the landscape, high on tomatoes and low on flair. But it was functional, and served as my main shopping facility. I gazed past the propped reels of chicken wire and roofing felt, and through the open store front. The sun had turned the main road into a baking concrete desert, the cement-forged apartment blocks sucking in the heat almost as greedily as the neighbouring greenhouses.

'Cos we have all kinds of lime. There's the sacks of powder, then there's the bags of slaked lime.' The hardware store owner was covered head to foot in a pelt of black hair. His moustache was a hearth brush. It twitched left and right, as though sweeping the words out of his lips. 'You're painting your house, right?'

47

'Erm, no. I'm building with it.' My shoulders drooped. I knew how inexperienced I looked. I had no idea what slaked lime was at the time, nor what difference it could make to anything. I was an eco- guppy flapping innocently about in a tank full of entrepreneurial construction sharks.

'Building with it?' The moustache brush made one large, incredulous sweep. With his tiny black eyes, and tooth-stuffed grin, the man bore a striking resemblance to Bluto from Popeye. The other two men in the store, both in flat caps, turned away from the coils of hoses they were investigating. They shuffled toward us. I was the most interesting thing this store had seen all week.

I stuck my chin out and did my best to appear knowledgeable. 'I'm making a house without concrete and I'm thinking of filling the foundations with a lime mixture.'

'Oh no no no.' The store owner shook his head gravely. 'Lime won't work in foundations. You can't build without concrete, dear.'

The two hose-browsing hillbillies also wagged their heads and mumbled their assent. A fourth man manifested from the store cupboard, younger and clean shaven. He peered at me from behind a bundle of watering cans. 'A house without concrete? What, like in the olden days?' he said. 'No. You can't do that. They get rats and damp and all sorts.'

'Got any wood-stripper?' Yet another older male entered the store blessed with an enormous beak of a nose. On seeing an animated discussion in process, he joined the group. We were gathering quite a crowd of spectators. The young assistant pushed a scythe out of the way and stepped into the circle. 'No, a house without concrete wouldn't be safe in an earthquake.'

'She wants to build an 'ouse wivout concrete?' The beak-nose butted in.

'Yeah,' said one of the hose investigators. 'She wants to use lime.'

'Fall down, it will,' the beak said.

This was the point my patience cracked. Because novice as I was, I still knew plain as day they were spewing nonsense. I stood up and brushed down my top. The five men moved back a pace.

'So if that's true, and if concrete's the answer, then why did all those apartments in Istanbul collapse so spectacularly back in 1999?'

There was a moment of silence. The store owner's pelt bristled. He inhaled. Then the moustache brush began sweeping in short, brisk strokes sending the words scattering into the corners of the shop. 'Because they weren't reinforced properly, and the foundations weren't deep enough, and they cut corners and didn't use enough

49

concrete. You can't build without concrete. We have plenty of it out the back. Just take cement bags instead. Fill your foundations with that!'

Why was I so adamant about not using concrete? Despite possessing no construction experience whatsoever, I had lived in many a concrete apartment, because Turkish cities are brimming with them. These cement boxes are not only soulless, but nasty damp ice-cells in winter. In summer they boil their inhabitants to a sweaty pulp. I knew from a frantic amount of research that Portland cement wasn't the tower of construction strength it was made out to be either, with a life of 50 to 100 years before deteriorating and crumbling. It is also notorious for wicking up water. I didn't want water seeping into my earth walls, it defeated the object. On top of this already sizeable heap of drawbacks, concrete happens to be the second largest contributor to the greenhouse effect, superseded only by fossil fuel consumption. And humans use an enormous amount of the stuff. In fact, the only thing we use more is clean water. So why then, were these self-proclaimed experts in the field so enamoured with it?

Concrete is big business. It's huge business in fact; on a par with oil. Turkey is no exception. Building codes and government quangos work in league with major cement manufacturers to create laws all but forcing people to use Portland cement. The folk on the ground believe what they are told. And thus the global cement mixer carries on turning.

So I didn't know what slaked lime was. I didn't know how much lime I would need. I'd never built any kind of foundation before, never mind with or without concrete. But, on the subject of Portland cement, I was better informed, and I knew it.

'My house will collapse in an earthquake if I use lime in the foundations? Is that what you're saying?' I addressed the ever increasing circle of onlookers. It was like a TED talk with hammers, axes and flowerpots as a backdrop instead of a studio. The crowd nodded. There was a low hum of debate. I stood a little higher on my imaginary soap box and pointed out of the window.

'Who's been to Rhodiapolis over there?'

Rhodiapolis was an ancient city about 20 minutes out of the town with amphitheatres and temples that had defied two millennia of earthquakes. A couple of the men hesitantly raised their hands. Bluto's moustache became very still.

'Is it still standing? Yes. Did they use concrete in the foundations? No.' I gathered myself for the finale, enjoying myself somewhat now. 'Know what they used?'

The circle of men were staring at me fascinated. Everything about the scenario was noteworthy. I was a foreign woman in a hardware store barking at them about ancient cities and cement. They had conversation fodder to chew over for weeks to come.

'...Lime. They used lime, my friends.'

A buzz of consent rippled through the group. Bluto raised a conciliatory eyebrow (I think he only had one anyway).

'I'm telling you, the government and its cronies are conning you, because they make a fortune out of selling you cement. They tell you to abandon your lovely mud and stone homes, and for what? For one of these hideous, concrete ovens? It's a tragedy! That's what it is.'

There was a rumble of animated conversation. The men folk began talking amongst themselves. I took the opportunity to escape and beckon the store owner outside. Once we reached the depot, we stopped.

'Which lime do I need then?' I gaped at the wall of dusty sacks.

'The hydraulic powdered stuff.'

'OK. I'll send a tractor to come and get it. I also need a trailer full of round gravel and four reels of thick, industrial barbed wire.'

'Barbed wire?' The various clumps of facial hair began twitching again. 'Whatcha gonna do with *that*?'

I slid Bluto a look of weary impatience. 'Let's just not go there today, eh?' I said.

He shrugged and called the young store assistant to prepare my supplies. Typically, it took hours.

It was while I was sitting in the hardware store again, drinking my third glass of tea and waiting for the tractor to arrive, I mused on the subject of building materials. I was surrounded by them. There were buckets of nails and screws, reels of plastic piping, roof tiles, paint, brushes, rollers, saws, scythes, drills, taps, washers, reels of rope, great rolls of plastic sheeting and shade cloth. All these bits and pieces had over time become elements of *The Way Things Were Done* in the building world. No one ever questioned them. Sons learned from fathers, apprentices learned from craftsmen, and the rest of the lay population accepted that these folk knew what they were doing. Yet who was it that first decided cement was to replace lime, and on what basis? Who deemed chemical paint so much of an improvement upon its natural equivalent? Who decided roof tiles had to be the flatter shape they are now, rather than circular as they used to be? How strange that the myriad possibilities for creating a shelter to live in has been constricted by what the average hardware store can sell us, and what the average builder has been taught.

Being a novice has its disadvantages. One is easily ripped off, and even the simplest task can be a case of reinventing the wheel. But, the advantage of having no building education whatsoever is that one isn't restricted by mainstream thought, by the mindless repetition of *The Way Things Are Done*.

***

It took Celal and me two days to dig our trench. We stuffed it with rocks, of which there are lorry loads on my land. In addition, I had ordered a trailer full of a special type of builder's gravel – smooth, round stones – to pour over the top of our rocky foundations. I was adamant they must be of the smooth, round type so as not to rip the earthbags that would sit on the top.

'When's the gravel comin' then?' Celal called out the next morning.

As something of a stone wizard, he was hunched in the trench filling in the gaps of the stone foundation. His nimble hands slotted the nobbled, white lumps of limestone in place. It was a large, rocky puzzle. I was pacing about my land waiting for the appearance of the gravel truck. The sun was already scorching the top of our heads, and the earth was a hard, baking slab.

'Oof I don't know. They said this morning, but what does that mean?'

Celal raised his head from the foundation channel, his face a filigree of sun-whipped experience. 'It means whenever they get their arses out of bed,' he chortled.

Over the next few days, one way and another, the gravel arrived. Now a tarp-covered fortress of lime bags guarded the entrance of my property. A speckled, grey dune of gravel spilled down from the road. The four hulking reels of industrial barbed wire poked ominously out from behind my tent platform, provoking looks of perturbed curiosity from all those who walked by them. But time was passing, and I had little of it. I had gathered my materials and my resources. With Google and a superbly helpful website called *Natural Building Blog* as my only advisors, I hurriedly prepared to make a few inroads into the world of house construction, and thereby subvert *The Way Things Were Done*.

The Earthbag Bible

The next week, by the grace of the god of mud house building, my dad came to Turkey. With him he brought a nice square package that I'd been waiting for with baited breath. It was a book; a guide to building earthbag houses, and it was soon to become my earthbag bible. As the autumn sun played on the sea, I sat with him and a family friend Betty on the beach. The pair of them were staked on sunloungers and from the spare-ribs-brown of their legs, they appeared to have taken a decent grilling. While they sizzled alongside, I edged under the shade. I opened the book frantically thumbing the pages concerning foundations.

This was the first, but by no means the last, time I doubted myself. The book was full of processes I didn't understand; strip anchors, joists, stem walls, capillary walls. When I'd asked the only other earthbagger in Turkey, my American friend Chris, it hadn't seemed as complicated as this. I moved off the chair to make models on the beach out of stones. I scratched my head. I fretted. In the end I couldn't stand it, so I decided to bother my dad.

'Do you think the foundations are deep enough?'

'Yeees,' said Dad to the sun. 'They'll be fine.'

'But the trench is only half a metre down.'

'Well, the church back in Wivenhoe hardly has any foundations. In fact, many buildings back home have footings not more than a couple of feet. You're not building a multistorey car park. It's a one floor mud hut. Go on, you'll be alright.'

I'd sit back on the sunlounger pacified for a moment. And then I'd remember my dad's attempt at repairing the phone. By the time he was finished, the phone had suffered a deep gouge down one side, was filled with blobs of Araldite and was thereafter forever bound together with electrical tape.

'But there aren't any earthquakes in the UK. It needs to be earthquake proof. Do you think making a stem wall from gravel bags will hold? Or should I fill them with some sort of lime-crete? Or...or?'

Dad moved a little more into the sun and chewed on a toothpick. Betty put down her novel, raised her sunglasses and turned to face me.

'I think, Kerry, you're just going to have to go for it, otherwise you'll be debating it in your head forever.'

Wise words. Lesson number two I've gleaned from the earthbag adventure is that while information and deliberation has its place, it really should be kept in it. I've seen far too many people who set up camp in the ideas phase of a project and never move out. They spend years discussing this way or that, this bag or that, this foundation or that. It's lethal. Nothing ever manifests. Better to build something and have it collapse, I'd say. At least you'd learn from the mistake. But as many have probably already discerned, I'm not exactly the most cautious person in the world.

Dad yanked his sun cap off and stared off into the horizon. The sun was gliding toward it, a golden phoenix moving in reverse.

'Can I have a look at that trench a minute,' he said stretching out a sun-blackened arm.

I handed him the camera. He pulled it to his face and flicked through my photo frames. A frown line began to stretch from one side of his forehead to the other. He found the picture of the trench Celal and I had so diligently dug the previous week and filled with rocks for drainage. I was pleased with the rocks, they'd worked well. Dad scratched his head.

'You did check it was level, didn't you? I mean, that's the most important thing, otherwise...'

I gulped. The roots of my hair stood to attention like a regiment of follicle health and safety inspectors. A vision of an earthbag house lurching forwards and plunging bobsleigh style the length of my slope rose like a phantom from a builder's nightmare. I sat up, yanked my phone out of my day pack and began dialling frantically. The phone beeped and beeped. Finally, it picked up.

59

'Aye.'

'Celal. Is that you?'

'Aye.'

'Can you come over tomorrow? I think we might have screwed up.'

New Recruits

We had forged a nice, neat stone ring for the foundations, and with the help of some string and some markers it was level. Now it was starting. We were building; however, I faced two significant obstacles, troubles that dragged my every effort through a gluey mire of extra labour: I had no power and no water.

Not having electricity means one can no longer rely on power tools. Everything, I repeat, *everything*, has to be completed by hand. The only tool I could use, if I charged it at Dudu's house, was my drill. Circular saws, grinders, sanders, welders – all were useless to me. Yet this was a piece of mud pie compared to the water migraine I was suffering.

I had no running water and no spring. Every drop of H2O I used had to be brought onto the land in my car. Each morning I'd drive two 20-litre plastic tanks 800 metres up the hill to the graveyard where there was a public tap. I'd fill up the tanks, stagger with them to the car, and listen to them slurp as I rolled and jolted down the broken, dirt lane to the house. It was a nightmare which turned me into something of a crabby, water-hoarding shrew.

'Here's your mug, Ahmet, and the purple one is for Esra. Don't put it in the washing-up bowl, because I have neither the water nor the energy to keep washing up every tea break.'

Two more recruits had joined the earthbag team: Celal's son Ahmet and daughter-in-law Esra. The young couple were something of an anomaly in a village of toothless tomato farmers and large-bottomed *gözleme* guzzlers. Both were absurdly good-looking. Ahmet with his blonde hair and his 1960s King of Cool persona was a veritable Steve McQueen, while Esra was the Kiera Knightly of Yapraklı village with a talent for whacking nails in hard and straight.

'Oh well, if I'm gonna be stuck with the thing forever, I want that white mug, cos it's the biggest,' said Ahmet holding the cup by the handle and peering into it unimpressed. We were gathered near what could loosely be described as my kitchen. In reality, it was more a collection of pots and crockery arranged on a dusty plank under an olive tree.

I sighed and handed him the white cup. Esra reached for the purple one. 'And be careful with water. If you need to wash your hands make sure you use that container over there,' I added a little impatiently.

'Alright, alright. Jeez, you're a bundle of laughs, aren't you?' Ahmet flashed his blue eyes at me, eyes that made all the girls in the village quiver. Blue eyes are a rarity in Turkey, and just like Mustafa Kemal Atatürk, the founder of the Turkish republic tattooed on his forearm, Ahmet knew how to work those baby blues. As an ex teacher, I could give pretty much as good as I got in the eye whipping department. Thus I smote him with one of my mid-range, jade-encrusted rapier stares. Ahmet cut me a rebellious grin, dropped the mug on the table and disappeared to the other side of the shed. I was suddenly swept back 20 years to my days working in the boys comprehensive in Barnet. I sucked the inside of my cheek and turned to the wooden table.

I was arranging the mugs, sugar, small carton of UHT milk and the hot water flask ready for the first tea break. On the edge of my field of vision, I could vaguely see Celal peeing in a bush next to the forest. By my side, Esra had rolled up her sleeves to reveal a tattoo on her right bicep. She was surveying my land, gauging it. I wondered what she was thinking. From an outsider's point of view, it looked like the whacky camp of a foreign nature nut. Irrationalities and eccentricities proliferated all over it. Why, for example, did I have a pretty, hand-decorated mirror hanging on a branch in the random space where my composting toilet was, yet no shower? Why did I spend hours aligning the rocks in a perfect curve on a terrace when I didn't even have a roof over my head? Why did I have three hammocks, but no bed? And why had I just planted jasmine and basil when I had no water? These were all paradoxes not easily answered by the mainstream mind. Esra, who had just married the village bad boy, cut her hair short and drove a motorbike, wasn't particularly conventional either.

'Ooh did you make this? Isn't it lovely?' She was fondling one of my hand-painted stones that she'd picked off the wooden table. Now who doesn't enjoy it when their creations are appreciated? I warmed to Esra in an instant. We were discussing how to paint a rock and which beach the best ones came from, when suddenly, there was a yelp. We both looked up, stones in hand. Ahmet's voice bawled from behind the shed. 'Oh no! I've just dropped the whole water container on the floor! It's pouring all over the place, going *totally* to waste.'

I closed my eyes. Not just my heart sank, everything sank; my lungs, my small intestine, my appendix. This meant I now had to rumble up the road again and refill the tank. I wheeled round, furious, ready to send Ahmet packing, and bellowed, 'You did *what*...?'

Then I saw him standing next to the water tank guffawing. 'Hahaha just kidding, Kerry,' he said pulling a yoghurt pot full of water from the container and raising it, as if to say cheers.

Esra snuck up next to him. She shook her head. 'Oh Kerry, you mustn't listen to him. He's *always* like this.' She gazed at him clearly besotted.

I swivelled my eyes to the sky. 'I can see the days are just going to *fly* by,' I muttered to myself in English as I clomped to the shed. I pulled out a pile of sacks and slammed the door shut. Thus the first morning with Esra and Ahmet commenced.

Our primary task that day was to set about building a stem wall. I'd never heard of such a thing before. According to the earthbag bible, the stem wall served one major function: it prevented damp from wicking up into the earth walls, and in a climate like Turkey's in winter, this is crucial. Holidaymakers to Turkey's southern coast would be forgiven for thinking it never rains. The Mediterranean region usually enjoys a solid 300 days sun a year. However, on those 50 odd days of cloud one certainly gets one's money's worth of precipitation. Some have pointed out it might be more appropriate to build an ark.

'Right, on the first two or three layers, we're going to fill the sacks with gravel.' I stood in the centre of the foundation ring waving a pair of orange sacks about like a semaphore signaller. Esra and Ahmet were standing next to me absorbing this weird new technique with curious scepticism. 'The gravel will create a stem wall that lets the water drain out and stops it damaging the mud walls above.' I preached as if I knew what I was talking about rather than paraphrasing what I'd read in the earthbag bible the night before.

'So is it two layers or three?' asked Ahmet as he stuck his nose tentatively in a sack.

'I don't know yet, I haven't decided,' I replied through gritted teeth.

'Concrete, that's what you need. Who's ever heard of a house without concrete?' Ahmet shook the corners of the sack.

I handed him a pile of 50 more and told him to get gusseting. Because most sacks are not gusseted on purchase, when they are filled with earth or stones, they lose their rectangular shape. While this isn't structurally problematic, it's untidy and results in a wall with multiple sack corners bulging out, and is a devil to plaster over too. This was why we were folding the ends in.

Celal sidled up to our group curious about the sack folding taking place. 'What can I do?' he said scratching his head.

'You and I can make a bag holder,' I smiled at him. I left the others knee-deep in polypropylene, and beckoned Celal to the tool shed. Pulling out a couple of broom handles and some nails, I turned and handed him the hammer.

'Bag holder? What's that?' Celal was shifting his feet uncomfortably.

I lifted the earthbag bible from its shelf in the shed and brought it outside. Flicking through the photograph-filled pages, I soon located the picture of the bag holder. I thrust the book in front of Celal. His eyes grew wide, either with wonder or angst, I couldn't quite tell. He stood silently for a moment contemplating the witchery of the diagram and how to leap from that to a three dimensional object. Sensing the rising panic, I handed him a broom handle.

'First you can saw this to size. Just let me get the tape measure.'

It took the best part of the morning, but in the end Celal and I constructed an openable and shuttable, wobblable and wigglable, utterly transportable bag holder. We displayed our work proudly to the rest of our team. Ahmet threw it a suspicious glance. Esra inspected it, fascinated. The point of the bag holder was to keep the sack open while it was filled with earth or gravel. We all had a bash at folding the sack edges over the holder, and everyone murmured in assent. It worked.

The day clicked smoothly through the gears from then on in. We divined how to close the ends of the bags with a nail and how to lay them head to toe. Esra and I placed the bags, while Celal barrowed over the gravel. Ahmet the Trojan filled the sacks and dragged them over to us. By late afternoon we had all but completed our first layer. It was thrilling to watch the circle manifest in the dirt, like seeing a ring of giant orange toadstools pushing their caps through the earth.

The migrating flock of afternoon shadows began to roost on the west side of the land. Our gravel circle grew darker and cooler. I grabbed a pullover. Esra zipped up her jacket. We had reached the final bag of the first layer. Celal and Ahmet dropped their shovels and ambled over to witness this auspicious moment in Turkish earthbag history.

'Kerry, you know we're going up in layers? Well, won't the bags slide off each other? How will we stick them together?' It was Esra who asked, and it was the most sensible question I'd heard in days.

'That's what the barbed wire is for.'

Esra stood up and peered at the heavy, spiked reels behind the tent platform. She turned back thoughtfully and flattened the gravel in the sack with a gloved hand. I folded the flaps over like a parcel, and she pinned it with a nail. Boom. Down it went. Celal clapped. Ahmet nodded in satisfaction.

The sky turned from forget-me-not blue to orange and lilac, with the great pines on the ridge cutting sinuous black paths into the light. Esra and Ahmet dutifully collected stray sacks and yoghurt pots, while Celal wandered round the orange ring, face rumpled in thought. He regarded the sacks warily, as though they were alien eggs that might at any time hatch into man-eating larva.

Esra pulled off the work gloves, while Ahmet grabbed his jacket. Then the Aksoy family said their goodbyes and traipsed up the track to their car. The new recruits were obviously tired. Yet no one looked bored. Tedium was not the name of the earthbag game. Everyone, including myself, was wondering, 'Can you really make a house out of a bunch of grain sacks? Is this *really* going to work?'

The Stem Wall

Esra, Ahmet and Celal Aksoy all lived together in a single-storey whitewashed house about two kilometres away in the village. And they weren't alone. They shared their home with a menagerie. There were flocks of ducks and chickens running free in the yard, six cats, three dogs, a sheep, a goat and a rabbit. Sometimes, just after the sacrifice festival, the sheep disappeared ominously and a month later another would arrive.

Celal had been born in Yaprakh but had moved to the city in his youth. He was one of many. A relentless government policy of urbanisation, cultural snobbery and media enticements would pull a nationwide stream of Celals from the Turkish countryside. The cultural gulf between the city and the country in Turkey is vast and gaping, and from the west to the east of the nation this gulf yawns into an abyss. While a city dweller in the west may be living much like their counterparts in the developed world, with mortgages, car payments, 9–6 jobs, traffic jams, school parents evenings and iPhones, in a remote eastern village they may be illiterate, committing 'honour' crimes, marrying their daughters off at 13 and carrying out blood feuds.

For too long, this devil-or-deep-blue-sea dilemma has been foisted upon the Turks as though there were no alternative. Generally, however, the city has failed the poor just as catastrophically as the Anatolian fields. In a way, it failed Celal too. He was nearly 60 and had spent his entire life working on building sites and hacking through manual labour jobs. Now he suffered lung disorders as a result of heavy smoking and pollution. But he was a grafter. From nothing, over the years he managed to claw together the money for a flat in Antalya. Once he retired, Celal returned to the village of Yapraklı where he had inherited land. It happened to be in one of Turkey's most pristine areas, Lycia. None of his family felt compelled to join him.

Having myself just scuttled out from the vice-like grip of the system, the Turkish worship of urbanity frustrated me on a daily basis. Since I had moved into a tent, my eyes had been opened to the fact that somewhere between or beyond the lustreless drudge of developed modernity and the brutality and ignorance of the underdeveloped rural poor, lies another option for the developing world, one that doesn't aid the agenda of the politicians and thus is largely concealed. It's independent, thrives off-grid, agriculturally abundant, healthy and free. Celal was one of the few who having seen 'the other side', knew which bank was greener.

'Aye!'

'Morning, Celal!' I cupped my hands over my eyes to see him trotting merrily down the slope, with Apo as usual bringing up the rear, ears flapping, tongue lolling. The sun was shameless for the season. Its gleaming fingers had just reached over the triangular tips of the pine forest, and they had the Midas touch. The entire slope had been cast in a gold so dazzling it made my retinas smart.

'Where are the others?'

'They're a comin' in the car. I walked cos I had some stuff to do at my hut before I came 'ere, feed the cats and the like.'

I nodded. Celal slowed as he approached the building site. He circled the first, almost complete layer of gravel-filled sacks. Kneeling, he prodded one of them his face visibly brighter than the evening before. He adjusted his cap and looked up at me.

'I reckon sgonna work,' he proclaimed, before standing upright again. He walked over to the wooden table and parked himself on a rickety stool.

I sat opposite him and raised both my brows simultaneously. 'What made you such a believer all of a sudden?' I asked, filling his cup up with water from a glass jug.

'Ah, I saw a documentary on the telly last night 'bout mud houses in Africa. They were round as well, lasted for years them houses did.'

We heard a rumbling. Ahmet and Esra possessed their own donkey-buzzard, only theirs was fire engine red. It groaned and creaked as it rolled painfully down my broken track. There was a squeal of brakes and a slamming of doors. An instant later, Yaprakı village's most handsome couple strolled onto my land.

With the sun white and livid above, all four of us gathered inside the orange circle, a coven of gravel-bag druids. Within minutes, the bag holder was open, a polypropylene sack was folded over it, and the stones were being shovelled in.

***

'Ooof!' Ahmet dropped another full sack in front of us. 'Know what?' he said. He was still bent double and looked up at me red-faced. 'This mud caper is never gonna work. The whole thing's gonna melt like a massive chocolate pudding when it rains. It'll be funny to watch though. I might bring a couple of beers and sit on Dad's land to spectate. We can sell tickets. Then you can earn enough money for a *real* house.' He stepped back and roared with laughter.

I stuck my tongue out and waved an orange sack at him. 'Just get shovelling, Ahmet.'

He walked to the centre of the circle, bent down and scooped up a spade-full of small grey stones.

'Don't worry, we'll let you kip in our house when it falls down. We're generous like that, me and Esra.'

Esra giggled. I groaned.

'You might have to share a bed with the rabbit though.'

'Ahmet, I swear, before the day is out I'll shovel *you* in one of these bags, nail you inside it and stick you in my wall.' I yanked the mouth of a sack open quasi-threateningly.

'At least *I* won't melt when it rains,' came the inevitable rejoinder.

This was to be the onset of what I can only term as a flood of local disbelief regarding the entire concept of earthbag building. Now credit where credit is due, while Ahmet teased me mercilessly, this was only to pass the time. In practice, he, Esra and Celal put their hearts and souls into getting that house up. But they were in the tiny minority. As far as the rest of the world was concerned, I was making a huge error in judgement. Barely a day would pass without someone stopping by to tell me exactly how my house was going to fail. Visitors would murmur and snort and explain how it would fall apart, collapse in a quake, turn to dust, or melt. The villagers laughed out loud, architects shook their heads in morbid incredulity, other builders raised eyebrows. Stories of various failed attempts at earthbag wound their way up my hill – the alternative lifestyler down in the valley who'd tried the long sausage bags but had never completed his dome, and the woman whose hired help quit under the strain of the work.

With the speed and desperation of someone whose survival depends on it, I realised I had to create not one but *two* stem walls; one for the house, and one for *me* to prevent my confidence from wicking up the daily deluges of negativity I'd listen to:

'*Olmaz.*'

'You can't, it won't work.'

'Impossible.'

'I wouldn't if I were you.'

'You don't know what you're doing.'

'You'll be sorry.'

Pretty much the only local exception was to be Celal. In the wake of the African mud hut documentary he converted to earthbagism with the zeal of any new proselyte. Whenever anyone mocked the idea, he would leap to my defence and explain that in the old days that's how everyone built houses and that I'd gone on the computer and found out all about it, and that I had a book with great pictures in.

Dudu, however, wasn't nearly as certain. That evening I popped up to her house to borrow one of her picks. She rushed out, her usually happy face riddled with anxiety.

Almost sobbing, she held her hands up to Allah in desperation. 'Oh Kerry, why didn't you make a little wooden hut? *Why?* Celal doesn't know how to make one of these mud sack houses or an earth round house or whatever they are. *No one* knows how to do it. Oh, what a *terrible* mistake you've made! What are we going to do? Winter is here. It's *here!*' I patted her shoulder (which just about reached my chest) and tried to reassure both her and myself at the same time.

All pioneers deal with naysayers. Other friends I know who attempted new construction techniques created psychological stem walls from their patience, humour or just by ignoring the misinformed wet blankets that snort and flop about them. Unfortunately, patience has never been my strong point. I suffer fools about as gladly as a sabre-toothed tiger suffers a rat. What I do have going for me is an inveterate disposition of contrariness. Natural building necessitates the use of whatever materials you have to hand. Psychological defence mechanisms are just the same. Contrariness has its downsides, yet when it comes to coping with naysayers, I can wholly recommend its efficiency. Before the winter was out, I was starting to feel like a walking raised middle finger.

This confidence would take time and a few small victories to develop, though. The first layers of gravel bags were rising quickly from the ground. Yet after the sun had set and my team vanished up the hill, the darkness quickly gobbled up the heat of the day. I retired to my tent alone as the nights stretched colder and longer. I would pull the drawstring of my arctic sleeping bag closed, while I read books with gloves on watching puffs of condensation leave my mouth. Bathing was all but impossible so I was a grimy uncomfortable mess. The sheer enormity of the task began to dawn on me. The mass doubt I was swimming in burrowed under my skin. The cold snuck into my bones. I had $5000 in the bank, we were already half way into November, and I'd only just begun the walls. Each night I found myself sharing my pillow with 'You'll *never* be able to do this'. And each morning I woke up with stomach ache. Then I made my first monumental mistake.

The Floor Fiasco

The difference between a floor and a foundation is that a foundation is what your house stands on, while a floor is what *you* stand on. We're all standing on floors of our own making, attitudes of our own creation that we could alter if we truly wanted. While foundations can't be removed without wrecking an entire building, floors can, one board at a time if necessary.

One of the ricketier and more rotten floorboards I was walking on, and one that badly needed changing, was the belief that other people must know more about building than I did. This wasn't entirely groundless. I knew almost nothing, after all. Yet, what I failed to observe was that despite their ever-flapping tongues and know-all lecturing, most other people knew next to nothing either. Nowhere did this become more apparent than the episode of the wooden floor.

The reason for the floorboard madness was founded on what I thought to be a firm premise. Floorboards are rectangular and my house is round. Thus I concocted a hair-brained scheme to lay the boards on to the top of the stem wall and sandwich them between that and the next layer of bags. I'd create a nice smooth circular finish this way. Well, it seemed a reasonable idea at the time.

Just for the record, to lay a beautiful juniper floor when you have no walls and no roof is probably the most ill-advised thing you could undertake in construction, other than forgetting a roof or omitting doors. It stretches faith in weather conditions and building time frames to ridiculous and frankly impossible lengths. One deluge of rain and that floor is ruined. Why oh why did I do it, then? And more to the point, why when I had an army of doubting Thomases whining at me at every turn, did not one of them mention it?

'Ah smells alright, dunnit?' said Celal, his face creasing happily at the prospect of everything going just right. 'Good wood this. Last forever it will, so long as you keep it dry.' My local carpenter had proudly procured top-grade juniper. It arrived at the entrance of my land in a trailer one fine morning. Ahmet and Celal were carrying off the beams and lining them up on rocks

I looked at the sky. It was a glorious day, the blue stretching uninterrupted from one side of the mountain tops to the other. There was no doubt about it, the weather was on my side. I was buoyed by sureness. I knew my land loved me and while I might have harboured deep-seated doubts concerning my ability to erect a house, I was confident that at the very least my little cell of Gaia was going to take care of me.

'Kerry, I think I'd better start putting the protector on the wood, don't you?'

Esra, who was wearing a mind-bogglingly tight T-shirt, looked at me. I nodded. She strode to the shed, whipped out a roller and began furiously coating the beams and boards. Meanwhile the rest of us set about the few remaining gravel bags of the stem wall.

'Hi there! How's it going?' A familiar voice called down from the track above the house. I was holding a full sack of gravel. Making sure I had the rim firmly in my grasp, I stared up to see a couple waving at me.

'Adnan! Annika!' I beamed the breadth and depth of someone spying life-savers approaching.

Adnan was a journalist. How he and I happened to be perched upon the same mountain in the middle of Turkish nowhere is beyond me, but we were. He was an escapee from the intellectual melee of Istanbul who'd fled to the wilds of the south to find some silence to write. He had rented a small house a kilometre or two away near the 'main' road (the main road in our area constitutes the only one with a spattering of tarmac, lest you be imagining a peopled metropolitan high street). Despite his name, Adnan wasn't Turkish. He was a Pakistan-born Canadian. My house was going to make a good eco story.

'We're a bit late, sorry about that. You know me, had a deadline to meet.' Adnan, trotted past the gravel heap and coils of barbed wire, his backpack bouncing on his shoulders. It was almost midday and the sun was glaring.

'And we've brought a snack. I'm not going to be starved again like yesterday!' Annika carried a tray of biscuits in front of her like an offering. Her cheeks were already turning pink, and her short blonde hair was spiky with perspiration.

Annika was a German scholar and in her twenties, something that 40-year-old Adnan was rather proud of. In fact, with his boyish frame, full head of jet black hair and his backpack, Adnan wouldn't have looked out of place on a skateboard in a high school yard, so there wasn't a disrespectable amount in visible years between them. The pair had met in the field in Pakistan. They were a couple often separated by their work; Adnan hunting war stories in the botch of beleaguered states lumbering between Turkey and Kashmir, Annika on research projects in Afghanistan or studying back in Europe.

We convened under the ropey thick trunk of my grandmother olive tree. With her tall branches stuffed full of foliage, she was by far the most generous shade on the land. It was this dear old tree that protected the plank of wood laid on stones constituting my kitchen worktop. 'I've booked my flight.' Annika rounded her shoulders mournfully as she handed me the biscuit tray. I accepted it guiltily. As an aside, should anyone ever consider earthbag building, natural building or any kind of building, there is one thing you need more than anything else: a cook. If I were to embark on such an adventure again, this is the first thing I'd change, otherwise your team is keeling over half-starved for much of the time.

'Really? You have to go already?' I said, now eyeing the biscuits hungrily.

Annika nodded. 'I have to finish a thesis for my masters, and I have so much to do back in Germany before I head for Kabul.' She eyed me through her glasses as I looked about for a plate that could more or less be accepted as clean.

'When are you going?' It's a terrible thing to admit. I was wondering how many days with an extra pair of hands I had.

'In a week.'

Oh dear. That wasn't very long. I plucked a frying pan from a branch in the holly bush and pulled the oil bottle from the holder its winding roots had created. My gas hob was perched on a small wooden table I'd found rotting behind a friend's house in the valley and repurposed. I lit the hob and threw the pan on the flame. Then I pulled out some eggs from my cool box which was only cool thanks to Dudu who froze bottles of water for me each night.

'Aye that's the *ezan* calling, must be lunch time I reckon,' called Celal from behind a small mound of earth he was digging. He threw down his spade. I groaned from my kitchen enclave. Looking at my phone I saw it was indeed

85

just past 12 o'clock. The other two mosques began to croon along with the first adding acoustic weight to Celal's claim.

'There's only one more bag left to go on this row. Esra and Ahmet, can you quickly lay it down? Then we'll break for lunch.'

The couple nodded, and then shovelled at speed, while Celal loitered by the fence. Adnan walked to the gravel-filled stem wall and patted the sacks appreciatively. Then he pulled off his pack, perched on a gravel bag and fumbled for his camera.

'Ah this house is gonna be just *awesome!*' he called over at me. I cracked the eggs in the pan and beamed. Along with Celal – who was more a born again earthbagger than a mud rationalist – Adnan was the other believer in earthbag in the region, and I clung to that gold nugget of moral support like an amulet.

'You think so?'

'Yeah. Look at it! Look at the goddamn view you're gonna have!'

I turned the gas off. Then I stepped out of the kitchen and walked over to the centre of the house circle. We'd just tacked a temporary door frame up. From inside the ring of bags I looked through the wooden rectangle out onto a vista of towering mountains and pine-decked slopes. The pomegranate fields in front had turned amber now that their fruit had been harvested. Adnan was right. It was bewitching. Briefly, I entertained a fantasy of reclining on an armchair in a mud house on a cold winter's day and reading a book in front of that view. The excitement rose in my chest at such speed I had to banish the vision lest I start jumping up and down on the spot.

***

An hour later, the Turkish posse returned replenished and upbeat now that we had company in the form of quirky foreigners. Annika, Adnan and I were fed and watered and focussed on forging ahead and laying the floor. How happily we all set to work that afternoon. What a crew! Six people, four nationalities and a fair bit of incomprehension. I hoped with a crowd like this we could make swift progress. The trouble (or saving grace, depending how you look at it) was that Adnan was something of a stickler.

'Erm, this isn't quite straight, Kerry.' Adnan was hunched on the floor clutching the spirit level staring at the grid of beams with grave intensity. I rushed over and peered into the glass box of the spirit level. The bubble was half in and half out of the lines.

'Ah, it's only a bit out. It'll be alright,' I said, not exactly conscious of the fact I was directly channelling my dad. Adnan's eyes snapped away from the level. 'Kerry, you can't just say it'll be alright. It might only be a millimetre out at

87

this point, but if we carry the line from the front to the back of the house that millimetre becomes quite a few centimetres.'

I wrinkled up my nose. 'Are you sure?'

Adnan clapped the spirit level onto the beam matter-of-factly. 'Find some string and I'll prove it.'

Annika, who had taken over from Esra on the wood coating, stood up roller in hand and raised an eyebrow. I huffed in defeat. It was one thing to deal with the baseless theories of naysayers, but quite another to discuss using the scientific method of hypothesis, experiment and conclusion. I wasn't going to be able to bluff my way out of this, nor merely stick my finger up and tell him to eat mud. I grudgingly wandered over to the shed to locate the string. Sensing dissent, the Turkish contingent began to look up from their tasks. Celal leaned on a wheelbarrow to spectate. Esra raised her head inquisitively. Ahmet decided now was a good time for a cigarette break.

We stretched the string from one end of the house to the other and confirmed that if I laid the wood on the stem wall it was going to be a few centimetres out. Adnan stood up and pushed a short lock of black hair back from his forehead. 'We need to lay strings for each beam, just to be sure we're level.'

I baulked at the prospect. 'That'll take forever!'

'Hey, c'mon. It pays to do it correctly, Kerry. This is *your* house. You're only building it once. You don't want a sloping floor, right?'

'What does it matter if it slopes a little bit?' I countered.

'But what about when you play marbles on it?'

'I don't play frigging marbles, do I? As long as it's flat enough for me to do a headstand, I'm happy.'

'What's going on?' Ahmet said, wandering back from his nicotine binge.

'Adnan says it's not straight,' I translated, eyes rolling.

Ahmet grinned. 'There ain't nothing straight nowhere on this house. The whole thing is wonky. It'll probably fall down anyway, so who cares?'

'Looks like we have a foreman,' said Celal with a cheeky smirk.

I shot Celal a stare cast in iron and took a call not to translate that. Celal coughed and returned to his digging. He was preparing a nice ring of fresh earth for us to bag later.

So, the upshot was, we spent a good hour tying bits of string from front to back along where the beams were to be laid. Celal and Esra meanwhile scoured the land for rocks to rest the beams on. Finally, we set about the laborious process of lining each beam up with the string, either by digging down under the rock to lower it, or finding a larger rock to raise it. Adnan rushed around brandishing the spirit level, leaping between the beams like a wood-hopping sprite.

'Level. Level. Level. Level. Ah...a millimetre out here,' he sang joyously as he skipped from one end of the circle to the other, oblivious of my quiet growling. The floor was going to be flat enough to balance eggs on.

'Eh! How's it going, neighbour? What are you doing today then?'

I pulled my gaze up ready to bite the head off whichever fool might be paying me a visit at this most inconvenient of times. Six people, and we were getting nowhere other than level. It was Dudu. She was perched on a high rock on her side of the fence from where she could view us all below. I called that rock, Dudu's observation tower. I didn't exactly tear her head from her shoulders, but she recognised the impatience in my look.

'Just thought I'd pop by and see how you were getting on. You need to get a move on, you know. Lucky for you the weather's held off this far. Ooh last year we had so much rain, the grass had started growing back by now.' Dudu adjusted her headscarf and looked Annika up and down. 'And who's this?' Annika had now moved from beam painting to gravel shovelling. She and Esra were filling up the orange sacks faster than Ahmet and Celal could lay them. We had begun the second layer of the stem wall. Unlike earth, the gravel wasn't particularly nice to work with. It was heavy, dirty work.

'This is Annika, Adnan's girlfriend,' I said. Adnan stopped his accursed measuring and puffed up a little. Annika waved in greeting.

'Look, Dudu, I wonder if you could do me a favour and put the tea on.' I was pushing my luck. In Turkey, asking your visitor to make the tea is akin to asking them to do your laundry. According to Islam, guests are sent from Allah (though personally, I was always more of the impression they were the devil's work).

'Tea?' Sure enough, a wave of shock was sent rippling over the wrinkled, brown terrain of Dudu's face, but she masked it quickly. 'Like that is it? Alright, show me where the teapot is and I'll take care of it,' she muttered.

Now we were seven people. But, as I was to realise over the course of time, numbers don't necessarily equal speed in getting the job done. Esra and Annika were troupers that day though, hurling gravel into bags like a couple of 19th century firemen feeding coal into a locomotive's boiler. Having shovelled gravel for the best part of the afternoon, Annika stood up and stretched.

91

'Adnan, I've worked far harder than you today. All you do is run about with a spirit level measuring.'

Amen to that! I thought.

'You are absolutely right, Annika dear, and I'll cook dinner for us all to make up for it.'

When I heard that I was impressed. In an instant all thought of spirit levels, tape measures and nit-picking task masters melted into the cream meringue anticipation of someone with a Pakistani heritage cooking me food. I'd been invited to dinner at Adnan's before, and it was always a taste bonanza.

The beams were eventually laid. We had drunk our tea. Dudu had wisely made a fast exit. I looked at the sky, which was something I'd grown very accustomed to doing over the months of living in a tent. Clock time is irrelevant when one is bedded down in nature's heart. What matters is where the sun is and how much daylight remains. Without power, my nights were long caves of blindness, which had proved a wholly rejuvenating experience. Once darkness descended, like the sparrows and the finches I had to find my roost and sleep. The sun became my consciousness. I woke with it and retired with it, falling in time with nature's light-dark beat.

With my face to the west, I read the sky. The sun had sunk behind the great olives long ago and the light had turned amber. We had less than an hour. The floorboards needed laying, but I knew they weren't long enough to stretch the full length of the house, because the carpenter had already warned me he couldn't procure wood that long. I began to drag the boards over the beams to analyse what I could do about this.

It was then, as sometimes happens, a stroke of divine inspiration struck. Now, there are pros and cons to having a wild imagination. I saw to my excitement that I could forge an attractive pattern out of the boards. I decided to set them in a large cross-like pattern and have some boards going horizontal, some vertical. It mattered little to me that this was a job for a professional carpenter. All I saw was something new and original and pretty, and I wanted it on my floor. There was only one hindrance. We had no power, and therefore no circular saw with which to slice the boards to the appropriate length.

I gathered the team. Six faces of varying hues stared back at me. Holding up a wooden board, I began. 'Ahem. So, we need to cut the floorboards. How are we going to do it?'

'Aye,' nodded Celal without much conviction.

There was some humming and hawing and shifting of eyes from right to left.

'I'll start on some. Perhaps we can share it,' offered Adnan magnanimously.

'Alright, we'll take it in turns,' I agreed (though frankly I was useless with the saw).

But we were interrupted. Ahmet had already pulled the hand saw from the shed. He returned to the orange circle, blue eyes flashing like a pair of Bunsen burners. Steve McQueen, the King of Cool, was coming to kick some construction butt.

'You lot measure them up, bang 'em down, and I'll take off the ends,' he said. It was the kind of job Ahmet revelled in, a save-the-world hero's feat of super-strength. I breathed deeply. There were something like 40 boards to be cut. Adnan opened his mouth, and then closed it. The corners of Esra's lips curled with pride.

I think Ahmet sawed continuously for a day and a half. And when I look at my floor, I always remember: 'Hand-cut by Ahmet'.

The Walls

After three days of construction work everyone was exhausted. People turned slightly ratty, motivation ebbed and the speed ground to a slow amble. So we took two days off. The floor was three-quarters laid apart from the edges, and I had covered it in a couple of sheets of polytunnel plastic. I was lucky the weather was dry, but what it lacked in rain it made up for in cold. The nights turned preposterously cool for the time of year and I slept in my jacket, two pairs of trousers with tights underneath, gloves, hat and arctic sleeping bag with a duvet over the top (I'm a Mediterranean lass and cold just isn't my thing). Over the course of the next two days, I visited friends with warm showers, wood burners and plug sockets feeling very much a heat and power scrounger. One of these good Samaritans – himself an experienced natural builder of the wood variety and a staunch rejecter of earthbag – warned me that perhaps it wasn't such a good idea to slot the floorboards directly into the walls as I might need to replace a board at some point, and I wouldn't be able to pry it out. This was a fair point, which was why, after all the bother, we didn't complete the floor then, nor squash the wood between the bags. Laying the boards at the beginning had been a complete waste of time.

All too soon our days of rest were over. I returned to my tent, shivered through the night and awoke at first light, teeth chattering. A brassy sun rose over the pine forest. Even in late November it was swatting my tent at seven. I wriggled out of the nest of sleeping bags and blankets I'd cocooned myself in during the night, pulled on my jacket and a pair of jeans, and unzipped the hatch of the tent to crash headlong into the day. I stuffed my feet into a pair of dilapidated hiking shoes and stumbled down to the small gap in the rocks and bushes I called my bathroom. Then, carefully pouring water from a bottle, I brushed my teeth and washed my face. Returning to the tent, I yanked out my yoga mat and located a clear spot of ground upon which to strike a few poses before the rest of the day invaded. I'd just sat up from a spot of relaxation when I heard a voice.

'Mornin', we're all ready to go now eh?' Celal had strolled onto the land with Apo the dog, who was as ever close on his heel and cocking his leg over any post or bush available. 'We've got the mud and the bags and the wire and the gang. Let's get started, tell me where I'm useful.' I noticed as he approached, Celal's face was twitching and he whiffed mildly of alcohol. 'We gotta get it right, all the village is laughing at us and saying the 'ouse will fall down, so we gotta get it right! I didn't sleep a wink last night you know, had to get up and have a tipple to set me straight.'

Celal had obviously taken the mud mission very much to heart. He had heeded a calling to fly the earthbag flag in Yapraklı village. I realised his pride was resting on my success.

97

'It's going to be just fine,' I bluffed. 'But I've got a few things to explain first.' I felt the responsibility of saving Celal's face in the community join the host of other earthbag worries jostling for room on my shoulders. The noise of a motor rumbled nearby. I heard tyres skidding and tripping over rocks. Finally, a car creaked to a standstill at the top of the land. Ahmet and Esra had arrived. Doors slammed. Cigarettes were extinguished. Then the pair of them trotted toward us.

'Bang on time!' I said. 'Morning you two. Everyone alright?'

The young couple nodded, still mute and puffy-eyed from the hood of sleep they'd just lifted.

'Right, we just need a bit more dirt, so we'll dig until ten, take a tea break and by that time Adnan and Annika will be here. After that, we're building a wall and it's going to be the most bad-ass boundary this village has ever seen!'

Ahmet snorted. Esra stared at me without blinking. It was true, I'd been watching far too many Hollywood movies of late. Well there was little else to do in a tent engulfed in darkness and cold by five pm. Every day, I would charge the laptop battery at Dudu's house, and if I was lucky I'd get an entire film's worth of power. If not, I'd have to chew my nails and wait for the ending the next day.

So we had reached the wall, and my first attempt at engineering a boundary. Boundaries are one of life's little jokes. Guaranteed to rouse conflict, they are wisdom's way of preventing us all from dissolving into a characterless soup of undefined mediocrity. Just watch anyone without clear boundaries; they are generally short on personality, lack conviction and, if I were to be slightly harsh, spineless. Borders exist because difference exists, and where difference hunkers down, you can always find splashes of disgruntlement.

As an aside, it's true I've experienced plenty of trouble with boundaries over the years; either I'm building walls thick enough for a nuclear shelter (take one step nearer and I'll shoot), or I'm throwing the doors wide open and yelling from the rooftop, 'Narcissists, please pillage my time and resources for I am a complete mug.' I have slipped from co-dependent to recluse and back again more times than I care to remember, and at the time of the earthbag adventure I had definitely dug out a nice deep bunker for myself on the hermit's side of the pendulum swing. If I could have possibly built that house alone, I would have. Agh, but I just couldn't! Even if I'd had two years to do it, I still needed help. So, much to my irritation, I had to allow others inside the project. These outsiders would pour their essence into the house I was building and change it, affect it – a misanthropist might say 'pollute it', a holist 'enhance it'.

The strange thing was just how much help I received. It was a miracle of sorts. The right people were always there at exactly the right time. They drifted to the land as though yanked there by some mystical earth magnet. Angels. My land was bringing me wonderful, dirt-loving angels. The only question was, would I let them in?

***

It was afternoon. I was standing on the rocky terrace in front of the door frame gazing at a pine tree at the lower end of my land. It was now illuminated in a criss-cross of sun-stroked branches, transforming it into an enormous nature-woven installation. With every inch the sun dropped, the myriad of curling arms seemed to twist.

Annika and Adnan had arrived. While Adnan inspected the morning's work, Annika had taken up sack gusseting. She was standing behind me chatting. 'Adnan has been researching earthbag houses all night online. He's *obsessed!*' Her English was excellent. I wrenched my head away from the arboreal sorcery occurring below to see her neatly folding the corners of a sack inwards.

'Well, that's good news for me. I haven't had a single soul to brainstorm this with,' I replied while adjusting our home-made wooden bag stand.

This was an unfortunate truth. It is one of the curses of pioneering anything. One doesn't have anyone to discuss ideas with. Celal, while lacking nothing in loyalty and conviction, loathed thinking about the mechanics of the operation. If I talked too much about the engineering side of things or gave him a task that involved initiative, he became panicky and upset. Ahmet (intelligently) didn't want a shred of responsibility and if I asked his opinion would invariably shrug and say, 'I dunno, *abla*. You're the boss.' Esra had a perfect grasp of the methodology, liked the challenge, but at that point wasn't confident – though that was going to change considerably before long. Everyone else I knew locally had simply condemned the project. Adnan was the only other person in the vicinity with an inkling of what the word sustainable meant and how to use a search engine. And while I chided him for his finicky nature, it was actually a perfect complement to my gung-ho trail-blazing (some might say recklessness). Too many Adnans and nothing materialises (he'd still have been measuring that floor to this day, if he'd had his way). Too many Kerrys and you have some serious health and safety issues, and a possible cardiac arrest.

The bag holder was open and waiting. There was a large, messy heap of gusseted sacks scattered on the ground. I'd collected three yoghurt pots. We had a moat of earth freshly dug by Celal that encircled the stem wall. We were ready.

'Right folks, we are finally about to start the earthbag wall,' I crowed to the group. We were becoming a tribe, a curious multi-ethnic, multi-lingual earthbag clan. Esra, Ahmet, Celal and Adnan convened in the centre of the circle.

'Yoo hoo!' Annika waved an orange sack over her head like a banner. The rest of the group cheered. Everyone was primed for earthbag wall action.

'Ah feel this guys! Mud is so much nicer to handle than that gravel,' said Adnan who was kneeling in front of the pile of dirt Celal had been heaping up for us over the past three days. 'Ah smell it. *That's* Mother Nature!'

Annika and I sat down, dug our hands into the rich, cool mud and inhaled. I swear, it smelt good enough to eat. The Turkish contingent looked on mildly bemused. Once we were all back on our feet, Esra attached one of our folded sacks onto the bag rack, Ahmet scooped up two yoghurt pots of earth and threw them into the sack. Those who suffer the misfortune of living in yoghurt-impoverished lands may wonder why we utilised yoghurt pots as scoopers. In Turkey, rather than an insubstantial saccharin-laced breakfast option for dieters, creamy yoghurt is served as a staple side dish at every main meal. It is probably the only substance which can compete with cement in terms of consumption per capita. Turks purchase it in 5 litre buckets much like paint is bought in a hardware store, which is extremely convenient when you are building an earthbag house.

So the earth was now nestling in the sack in front of me. I stood and read aloud from the earthbag bible like the Priestess of Mud.

'Now you need to hard-ass the ends with the tamper.'

'Hard-what?' said Adnan.

'Hard-*ass*.' I made a point of stretching the 'a' in a parody of a North American accent. 'I'm just paraphrasing. That's what it says here. In fact the whole book is full of innuendo. We double-bagged the gravel for the foundations, for example.'

Annika snorted. Adnan shook his head. 'Are you going to translate that?' he asked, a merry little twinkle jumping from his eye. Never one to shy from the potentially bawdy, I translated. Celal was most impressed with the description. 'Aye hard-ass, gotta whack the bag on the butt right?'

'Celal says you've got to whack the bag on the butt,' I translated to Adnan deadpan.

'Is that before or after I double-bag?' he replied winking. I leaned over and showed him the picture. Adnan found a small tamper we'd made from a concrete-filled flower pot, stuck it in the bag and rammed all the mud into the corners to give the bag a square bottom.

'OK. Fill up the rest of the bag. We need exactly five-and-a-half more yoghurt pots of mud in there.'

'How many?' said Ahmet, awaiting the Turkish translation.

'Fave and a heef,' Adnan replied in broken Turkish. Ahmet blinked and swallowed. He bent down.

'One, two, three, four, fave, there you go brother, fave and a heef.' Ahmet thrust the bag at Adnan and grinned.

'Hey, hey I'm learning, I'm learning,' Adnan cried in feigned consternation. We all laughed. It was going to be a good day.

Earthbag building basically proceeds as follows: a ring of earthbags is laid. Then the bags are tamped (squashed) using some sort of smooth, heavy block. This flattens the wet earth so that it forms a solid brick. When in a few months it dries, it's as hard as concrete. As you tamp, each bag is squeezed into each other bag until there's no space left between them forming a solid mud circle. Once the tamping is complete, two rings of thick barbed wire are placed over the top.

In a normal rectangular house with straight walls, the weak point is the middle of the wall. Walls collapse from the centre. When you create a round house with round walls however, something rather magical happens. There is no weak point in the wall. On impact, each bag in the house absorbs the pressure equally. It's one holistic unit.

As the first layer of earthbags thudded one by one into place, the team began to find its feet. Celal was chief digger. Esra and Ahmet filled the bags, Adnan and I placed them and checked they were level and sitting properly. Annika was filling extra bags, or taking over when someone was tired. There's nothing quite as exquisite as being part of a work team when the project is flowing. It's like playing in a symphony or being part of a dance troupe. A wonderful sense of well-being pervades. And at the end of the day, when the sun casts its final shadows and the hills turn grey and indigo, satisfaction rises like steam from a teapot on an open campfire.

Being part of something is primal. It's who we are.

The day drew to its inevitable close with the North Star flicking off the lights and ushering us out of our dirt office. We had managed a row and a half of earthbags in an afternoon. Our arms burned, our backs ached, and we all but staggered up the track to our respective cars. But everyone was alight. We were biped flesh and blood lanterns. Because it was happening. I couldn't quite believe it, but we were building a wall!

Annika and Adnan had invited me for dinner. Why? Because I was bedded down in a freezing tent without power, and they were generous, kind and open. In fact, I was never wanting for dinner invites. Celal, Esra and Ahmet invited me frequently, Dudu almost every day. I would never starve, nor freeze to death because for some reason or no reason, whether I deserved it or not, people seemed to be looking out for me. This was especially unexpected as I'd spent the past six months avoiding humanity. I had secluded myself on my plot much as a hermit might, because I wanted to discover a place inside me that civilisation hadn't corrupted, the real me, the *natural* me.

It does seem when you abandon 'the niceties' of social interaction with its insipid expectations, when you stop caring what others think and forge ahead with something you love just for the hell of it, doors fly open, opportunities spring out of nowhere and help floats toward you like a cloud of mosquitos on a summer's night.

As I slammed the door of my car, Annika by my side and Adnan perched on the back seat, my cheeks tingled. A sweet warmth spread through my chest. It was a feeling I was experiencing often of late, especially at dusk; a wild concoction of enchantment and joy. I remembered the sensation from childhood gallivants into the woods, or den-building escapades or playing PomPom 123 with the neighbouring kids in the street when I was eight years old. This house-building adventure had begun as a survival mission, but was turning into a gigantic, muddy party. I was having a ball. Sometimes I thought the fresh air of the wilds was carrying tiny invisible happy seeds. Perhaps we inhaled them during the day as we worked and they'd bury into our lungs and sprout. By evening they'd have blossomed into a rainbow of ecstasy flowers. Forget the pill. It's no more than a cheap squirt of chemical gratification by comparison. The natural state of joy a human is capable of is beautiful. Nowadays, it's what I live for.

Adnan's house was located a little past the local graveyard. It was a typical one storey village cottage, with a tiled roof and concrete walls; draughty, utterly uninsulated and in all honesty not much warmer than my tent. He was renting it from a local who'd moved to the nearby town to work and he was being fleeced somewhat on the price, but it was a great summer retreat in the middle of nowhere, and somewhere he could write in peace.

My car steamed past the scattering of wonky gravestones rising behind the cemetery's stone wall. The three of us bounced in time. We turned into Adnan's road, which wasn't in much better condition than mine, and lurched into the darkness. A little way down on the left was a towering cypress tree choked by a viper's party of creepers. It was a tree which gave me the veritable heebie-jeebies. There was something about its statuesque lightless canopy and its dark, leafy hands that made me shudder. Something was in there, I was sure. We drove under it, and as always I shivered.

I pulled up to the rear of the cottage and turned off the engine. Three doors creaked open before slamming heavily shut again. Adnan, backpack dragging from his shoulders, walked briskly to the front of his house. He opened the metal grille of his door and stepped inside. Annika followed suit. Pulling on a woollen hat, I loitered outside. I noticed a freshly forged ring of grey rocks obviously serving as the fire pit. Picking up a few sticks from under the great almond tree at the front, I snapped them for kindling and then formed them into a twig tepee. There was no moon. The night sky was an arcane message of stars and planets.

Soon the fire was snickering and spitting like an exorcised demon. The flames reached out from the wood, delirious. I felt the Other World, the world of the Outside, the Unknown and Unknowable, licking my cheeks and forehead. It was a harlequin of firelight. A trickster. And it danced and tripped over the ground and the walls, while I scavenged for more wood.

'Whoa! What a fire!' Annika called out from the door, her head punching a black hole in the rectangle of orange house light behind her. Then she trotted down the steps. She was swinging something in her hands. I peered closer. It was a hula hoop decorated with metallic tape.

Standing by the fire, she held the hoop in front of her. She rotated it left and right. Then she began to turn it like a steering wheel. It appeared the hoop was hovering in mid-air while her hands were sliding round its edge. The hoop then seemed to leap onto her arm of its own accord, spinning around it as though possessed. The gossamer drape between illusion and reality twitched. Then the hoop clattered onto the ground.

'Agh! I can't quite get that move right,' she said, her face striped orange and yellow by flame.

'What are you doing? What *is* that?'

'Ah it's a performance art like juggling,' Annika replied.

I knew she and Adnan were both into circus, but I'd only ever seen Annika blazing trails with poi before. Adnan was a contact ball man. Contact ball is an unusual performance art and the closest I can think of to a juggling magician. Contact balls are often glass and made to move over the body, almost as if alive.

'Want a go?' Annika handed me the hula hoop.

I held it, listened to her instruction, tried it and failed. I tried again. Useless. I didn't bother with a third attempt. It was like contact ball, a skill requiring dedication and practise, and I simply didn't have the patience for it.

With the night a cauldron of secrets enticing us over to the other side, Annika continued hooping, while I poked the fire. Soon enough, Adnan scuttled out of the house holding a tray of fish. 'OK. It's barbeque time!' he cheered. I shook my head in amazement. Where *did* they get their energy from?

The Ghost Story

Annika left. We had now chugged merrily to the end of November. It was nothing short of a miracle that the rain had held off. The floor was covered in a plastic tarp, but it would only take one storm to wreck it. The pressure was now on to move up the wall. When we were left to our own devices, the earthbag team was motivated and productive, whacking those bags in place like a cohort of Turkish pizza makers throwing dough on a worktop. If only the outside world would let us get on with it! People were now descending upon us on a regular basis, sent by the devil as usual. I hated this gaggle of useless, tea demanding, tongue-wagging visitors whose only true motivation for turning up was to try and see what I was doing wrong so that they could 'mansplain' about it.

'When this house is done and looking just awesome, we're gonna invite round every naysayer in the valley. There'll be a bag of dirt at the gate, and they'll have to eat a cup-full if they wanna get in,' said Adnan. We were up to our armpits in wall and had begun adding details like plastic pipes for coloured glass sun catchers.

'Yeah, let them eat dirt,' I agreed happily imagining a line full of onlookers sipping from soil-filled mugs. We tipped a full earthbag onto the plywood runner. Adnan lifted its 'bottom' and I yanked out the runner. Then we both slapped it into place.

'Six. We need a sixer,' called Adnan to our bag fillers Esra and Ahmet crouching next to us in the dirt. They scooped the wet mud into their yoghurt pots and hurled them one by one into the next sack.

We were all grafting. Everyone sensed that time was of the essence and everyone knew what they were doing. I watched Esra in awe, her tattooed arm muscles flexing as she powered the earth into the bags. She was fast, focussed and possessed a seemingly inexhaustible well of stamina for a lass with a body that even the style nazis at *Elle* magazine would have accepted. I was inspired by her. Ahmet, on the other hand, was our own personal Hercules. Our concrete tamper failed after one round of earthbags. Adnan had found a massive marble birdbath lying around at his house, and I'd driven it down in the car. Somehow Ahmet lifted the thing and pounded the entire row of bags down, mostly single-handedly. When he wasn't around, both Adnan and I tried it. We managed about three drops each before collapsing.

Celal simply dug and dug and dug, and he was as happy as can be while that spade was in his hand. He would trundle up the path with the barrow, fill it up and return, with Apo trotting loyally behind. Adnan and I laid the bags. Adnan was the quality control of the project. 'We need to find the centre. If the bags are all lined up it will weaken the wall. Find the centre guys, *find* the centre!' He became known to the Turkish contingent as *mudur*, or supervisor. I, on the other hand, seemed to be making motivational speeches in perpetuum. 'Come on folks, one more round, we can do it!' and buying chocolate and beer. I was *patron* (the boss).

Sure enough, the wall began to rise.

Every organism possesses a wall, from the smallest cell membrane to the thick hide of a rhino. Walls are for protection, barriers to keep the inside in and the outside out – at least that's how I'd perceived it, and how most people perceive it. At that point in my life I felt I needed protection; from the elements that were growing colder and wilder by the day, from curious chatterboxes, from gun-toting hunters, from noise, from the World At Large. It has to be said, if it's protection you crave then earthbag walls are as good as it gets. They are bulletproof, soundproof, earthquake-proof, fireproof, hurricane-proof, bombproof, and almost impossible to knock down when impacted by say a car. They are boundaries. Good, solid, no nonsense, state what you get boundaries.

Ahmet had just dropped the next sack onto the runner, when we heard a jeep rolling down the length of my track. 'Now who's coming to waste our time? Hell, I wouldn't mind if they were actually visiting to be helpful,' I growled.

Adnan shook his head. Celal's eyes lit up. Unlike me, he loved visitors. Any excuse for a chat was good news to him. The jeep parked in front of my car. Three people emerged from the vehicle; an older German woman with someone who was obviously her younger Turkish lover. And my nemesis, Kemal. My stomach lurched. Oh God, what did the troublemaker want now?

The three of them wandered past the bags of lime and the compost heap, and said their hellos, Kemal swaggered as he approached the orange wall. I grudgingly offered them a glass of tea. They wisely turned it down. They looked about the ring of bags sceptically. The younger man fondled the earthbags curiously. The woman chatted politely.

'I don't believe it!' whispered Adnan, next to me.

'What?' I asked.

'Look at that guy. He's trying to push the goddamn wall down!'

I snuck round to have a look, and sure enough, there was Kemal, casually leaning into the wall to see if it would topple.

'Hey Kemal, it's looking good, right? Don't worry, people have driven trucks into these walls and nothing has happened,' I called out enthusiastically. He snapped to attention, face flushing. He refused to admit the wall was invincible, in fact he refused outright to reply at all. He looked very much irritated that my house was working. It was one of the many times I'd see vexation in the faces of those who doubted me. They just wanted to be right, but they so obviously weren't. I saw him reach into his pocket for a cigarette.

'Erm, smoking's not allowed on the land, you'll have to puff up on the hill next to the car.' Kemal knew this already, because everybody knew it. Now he was even more annoyed. He stomped up the pathway in silence.

I had five main rules on my land. 1. No smoking. 2. No killing. 3. No concrete. 4. No verbal abuse. 5. No straight lines. They were all incontrovertible apart from the last one. I simply wasn't a skilled enough carpenter to create wooden structures without straight lines. But the other four were immutable. Transgressions would result in the offender being sent off the property, probably never to return. I mused many times how curious it was then, that despite this overt display of totalitarianism and outright bitchery, I nonetheless had so many visitors and helpers. Sometimes I felt I was beating them off. Which just goes to show; in general people respect boundaries, though some will always try to give them a push, just in case they find a weak spot.

Kemal wandered back down the path a little, cigarette still burning. I eyed it ferociously. His eyes narrowed slightly and he threw me a not altogether pleasant grin. I felt my heartbeat step up a notch. Something was coming, I could smell it. I ignored him and carried on laying my earthbag.

'How'd you buy this land then? Only locals can buy here, and you're a foreigner.'

I adjusted the earthbag. Adnan pulled it into place. Then I turned and allowed a most beatific smile to flutter over to Kemal. The glory of knowing you've won a fight before it has begun.

'Ah well, you see although I may look like a foreigner to you, I'm actually a Turkish citizen.'

'Whatcha mean? How'd you do that?'

'Oh I paid my dues, don't worry. Once upon a time in far off yonder in another life I married a Turkish man.'

Kemal's eyes narrowed. He filled his cheeks with air and then expelled it in one noisy sigh. 'What happened to him? Pah, bet you dumped him the minute that ID card was in yer hand!'

I chuckled at that. Glancing over my shoulder, I saw the Turkish posse were doing a convincing job of pretending not to pay attention to our conversation, while filling earthbags and simultaneously straining for each and every word. Adnan was oblivious as the conversation was in Turkish. He was circling the wall and peering studiously into the spirit level. The German woman was now sitting at my wooden table gazing into space with her lover.

Kemal sidled up a bit closer. I moved a step back. 'So why don't you get another man?' he said. 'You can't live here without a husband. It's dangerous. I mean aren't you *scared?*' He threw me a look that was the disfigured lovechild of sleaze and threat. This was a make or break moment, the point in time where destinies are carved. One of the advantages of age is one becomes increasingly adept at spotting these moments and responding appropriately.

'Oh marriage is not for me. I'm happy as I am thanks. Besides, I'd pity the guy. As you know, this area is haunted.'

Kemal's expression shrank. 'Whatcha mean *haunted?*'

'Well, you must have noticed...the men don't seem to last long around here?' In fact, this was a disquieting truth. There had been two untimely deaths of males on either side of my land in the past five years leaving my area governed peculiarly by three single women. I was the only one who wasn't a widow.

I watched Kemal's cheeks pinch paler. The silence was palpable as Esra and Ahmet dropped their semblance of disinterest and avidly imbibed the conversation. But Celal let his shovel fall to the ground with a clatter. I turned to see him scowling. 'Oh don't start going on about that again, Kerry!' he shouted crossly. His face jerked uneasily.

'But *you* were the one who told me the story about Hatice the shepherdess,' I protested. 'You even told me this was called *The place Hatice was slain*.'

Now I had everyone's attention. Even Adnan and the German woman could tell something was afoot. Kemal had turned away, but his friend's eyes were popping like those of the fat, warty toad currently squatting under my platform. 'Hatice? Who's Hatice?' the young Turkish man said.

Celal, unable to resist the kudos of being both keeper and disseminator of such a ghastly secret, swelled in the limelight. He took his cap off and straightened his back. Then he rolled his hand up, held it in front of his mouth, and cleared his throat. Everyone edged closer to him except for Kemal, who had his hands in his pockets and faced Dudu's pomegranates in taciturn denial. But his ears were pricked to attention, I could tell.

Celal spoke quietly, 'The story goes, years ago, long before us...'

'How long ago?' My eyes bored into him, as though I might spot the tale somewhere inside him on its journey to his lips.

'Ooh, like nearly a hundred years ago I spose. May be less may be more. Anyway, there was a shepherdess, and while she was driving her goats somewhere in this area, she was murdered.'

Everyone gaped, bottom lips flapping like headscarves on a wind-lashed brow. The young Turkish gigolo shuffled his feet. Ahmet's cheeky smirk dissolved. Esra's eyes fixed onto the hill opposite, but she was paying scrupulous attention to every word.

'How? I mean how was she murdered?' I huddled in closer to the group surrounding Celal. I'd heard the story before, but it still made me shudder. Even so I was eager for more details.

'Dunno,' answered Celal with infuriating abstruseness. 'But that's why they call it *The place Hatice was slain.*'

Kemal turned from the pomegranates looking a little morose. 'Yeah, I've heard of that name. Didn't know it was around here though,' he said quietly.

A stillness descended upon the land. It seemed even the birds had been muted. The pines stopped rustling, the olives held their knotted tongues, and the rocks sat impassively, neither giving anything away nor taking anything back. I looked over the slope, fresh shoots poking through the dry remains of last year's grass. I wondered whether the land remembered that event. Was there blood trickling somewhere under this pelt of weeds and stones? Or was this just a local horror story created to animate a dull winter's night? My land had never felt in the slightest eerie to me. I had no intimations of the macabre. The plot felt magical and bounteous and giving. Perhaps Hatice had been murdered somewhere else nearby. Perhaps not at all.

Yet. Yet...

'Alright, time to go,' Kemal called his two guests. The German woman's face crumpled in bemusement. She had no idea what the discussion had been about, but the group's body language must have been striking. She and her terrified looking boyfriend trailed Kemal quickly out of the land.

Once we'd heard the jeep's engine start and its wheels crack the stones, everyone returned to their jobs, albeit rather quietly. Adnan had picked up a plastic water pipe and was waiting on the west side of the wall.

'What was all that about?' he said, as I returned to my earthbagging post.

I prefaced the explanation with, 'Now don't be alarmed...'

Naturally, Adnan's eyes widened when I said that. But as a war journalist, he'd spent plenty of time staring down the wrong end of Kalashnikov rifles in the Middle East, so he wasn't particularly easy to scare. Plus, he was a rationalist with no time for unquantifiable superstitious mumbo jumbo.

'Do you like ghost stories?' I asked as the next earth-filled sack hit the runner with a thud.

'Ah yeah, sure, I love them,' Adnan said grinning.

**

The next day, Celal was squatting on a rock nursing a cup of filter coffee (he loved filter coffee). 'Aye, know what they call you in the village?' he murmured.

'What?' I asked warily.

'Brave. Stubborn and brave. And a little bit mad to boot.'

I screwed my hand up and gave the air a little punch. I couldn't have created a better protective ring around the area if I'd circled it with an electrified fence and watchtowers.

Different Perspectives

It was all going smoothly. The walls were rising fast. We'd arrived at the windows in three days. With those thick cave-like walls, I had decided I wanted a lot of windows, and a south facing front door made of glass to suck in the sunlight. And a view. I wanted to sit in that circle of earth like the Queen of Mud, and survey the world. At night, that world was an inky landscape of distant lights that twinkled and pulsed in a golden arc. In the day it was an amphitheatre of emerald and olive folds. My eye was to follow the swerving dirt road through the pines all the way to a splodge of shimmering sea far away. It was to be the perspective of an eagle.

Perspectives fascinate me. Having moved from culture to culture, the arbitrariness of ethics, traditions, social etiquette and ways of looking at the world has been absorbed osmotically into my bloodstream. In one place (say Wivenhoe waterfront) it is polite to smile at a stranger as they pass, in another (Yapraklı village) it might be viewed as a come on, in another (the London Underground) you may be considered a psychopath. Perspectives are never divorced from the ground upon which they sit, and thus they warp and morph with every move we make.

From the perspective of many people, my life appeared a living hell. No power, no water, no house, no fridge, no TV, no washing machine, freezing my butt off under a 2-by-2 square of canvas. Two years later, a friend of mine made a documentary about me and my house and called it 'Living the Dream'. Her film teacher watched. 'Well, I suppose a nightmare is a kind of a dream,' he said. He was commenting from a concrete building in a large city and thus just couldn't see my perspective. Yet, those who came to the land, for the most part, were touched by it. Even those who thought I was barmy. Dudu's son-in-law and daughter turned up for tea one day. As they sat at the edge of my mud building site next to my open-air tree 'kitchen', the son-in-law said, 'Ah, I see why you don't want power. Don't get it. It will spoil it. It will change everything. It's so still here. So peaceful.' He was now viewing it from another perspective. The perspective of unadulterated nature.

'Hey there, I'm back!'

It was Adnan. He was standing at the lip of land at the back of the house, and from there he had a bird's eye view of the construction. He nodded and held up a hand with a raised thumb.

'Looking good, guys, looking good.'

Ahmet gaped up from his tamping, dropped the marble birdbath onto a bag and wiped his forehead. '*Mudur!*' he called out, 'Thank God you're back, this house ain't never gonna make it without you measuring up.'

'You're just on time,' I yelled at him. 'I need a pedant. We've reached the windows.'

To be more precise, we'd reached the window *frames*. Adnan trotted onto the land and dropped his bag on a rock grinning. 'Windows eh? Bring 'em on!'

So I brought them on. Eight pieces of wood to be banged into two squares. While our team of four carried on earth-bagging, he measured the wood, sawed it and nailed it together. Soon enough we had our frames. But they weren't going to work. In fact they were going to be a disaster. We had no idea about that on this glorious sunny day though. They looked nice and square and seemed to sit snugly on the wall. Thus, we blithely continued packing earthbags around them.

The team worked. Afternoon slid too quickly into evening. The sun evacuated the land and the shade it left in its wake was surprisingly chilly. Celal, Esra and Ahmet waved their tired goodbyes and drove off up the hill. The shade thickened into a heavy, cold dusk. Adnan was wandering about the house checking if we'd found our centre, and if everything was holding up as it should. I was collecting spades, picks and yoghurt pot mud scoopers.

'Adnan, can I ask a favour?' I said meekly as I yanked shut the tool shed door. I hate asking for favours.

'Sure!'

'Can I take a hot shower at your place? I stink.'

'Kerry, you don't need to ask that! You can use the shower any time you like. *Ya*, come for dinner, why not? I'll make us a vegetarian madras, what do you say? I'm sure you need to power up your computer.'

What could I say? Someone turns up, works his arse off all afternoon to help you get your house finished before you freeze to death, and then cooks you vegetarian madras. I gathered a towel and some clean clothes. We stepped aboard the donkey-buzzard and I 'floored it' up the slope to Adnan's little house on the hill.

As we rattled and rumbled down Adnan's track, and under *that* tree, for the umpteenth time I shuddered.

'Don't you think that tree is creepy?'

Adnan craned his neck back to look at it. 'It's a beautiful tree, that!' he said.

'But it's so dark and tall and all those vines crawling all over it...'

'Yeah, and? *I'm* not seeing it as creepy.'

I shrugged. We turned the bend and I parked behind the cottage.

Inside, the house, being predominantly made of concrete, was displaying its usual talent for absorbing the cold while ridding itself of heat as though it were toxic. Adnan disappeared into his room. I pulled some sticks from a crate, tore up a teabag box and threw them into the mouth of the wood burner. Then I lit the bundle of kindling and listened as it began to chug. Standing up, I stretched. Once the fire was roaring, I opened the door to his squat toilet. A small electric shower was pinned against one of its walls. Turning it on, I let the water heat while I undressed. Hurriedly I showered, shivering all the way. When I came out, Adnan was clearing up his kitchen. I blinked at the sight of it. The sink was filled with a crooked tower of crockery, like a pot and pan version of Jenga.

'Tell you what, I'll wash, you cook. I *hate* cooking,' I said.

An hour later we were both crouched in front of our computers, feasting on curry. I was throwing spoons of basmati rice into my mouth like it was dirt going into an earthbag. Adnan was engrossed in his screen. I flicked open a tab to check the weather. As the seven-day forecast opened up, I emitted a small sigh of relief. No rain anywhere on the horizon.

'Ah, thank God for that. Sun, sun, sun, I can't believe how fortunate I am with the weather!'

'Yeah, seriously. Can you imagine if it rained? Those floorboards, my God I don't wanna even *think* about it!'

I lifted my head and nodded.

'And *maan!* Ahmet sawed all those boards. You've gotta hand it to the dude, he's an ox.' Adnan spoke distractedly. The beep beep beep of a Skype call cut him off.

'Ah Annika my love! Hey there, how's it going?'

'Adnan? Is that you, Adnan?'

'Yeah, Kerry's here for dinner. We've just done the windows and it's looking great!'

I turned back to the screen. Suddenly I noticed something that petrified my heart mid-beat. I took a second glance at the temperatures. No. It was impossible. It never ever goes below freezing on the Mediterranean. We have no frost. No snow. Well, perhaps once every 15 years or something.

'Shit!'

'What?' said Adnan, with Annika joining the chorus virtually.

'Tomorrow night, it's going down to minus one!'

'Hey, that's OK. You can sleep here, we've got a spare room,' replied Adnan charitable as ever.

'I'm not worrying about *me,*' I wailed. 'It's the earthbags!'

If there's one weather condition you should not build earthbag in, it's sub-zero temperatures. The earth inside the bags goes in wet, and over a few months dries and sets. If the building freezes before the earth has a chance to dry you will be left with a wall full of powder. Normally, earthbag houses are built in the spring to avoid this risk, and then left to dry in the summer. I hadn't worried about it because Mediterranean Turkey just doesn't freeze. I pushed the screen away. All of a sudden I felt sick. Jumping to my feet, I strode to the door. I wanted to retrieve the earthbag bible from the car. I carried it everywhere, as I was only ever a page or two ahead of where we were actually building.

Two minutes later, I shut the door of Adnan's wind tunnel and loped over to the table. Sitting down, I opened the book. Adnan and I poured over the glossy pages shaking our heads.

'Let's check Wunderweather, I trust those guys. They have an hourly satellite picture. May be Accuweather made an error.' Adnan was clutching at straws. He began clicking his mouse. I was slumped in the corner with a terrible feeling rising in my belly. It mixed badly with the madras. Adnan raised his eyes from the screen and blew out his cheeks.

'It's going down to minus two the day after. We're fucked, man!'

'Buggered,' I added collapsing against the wall, and then sitting straight up again because the wall was so damn cold. 'It's doomed. The house is doomed. And so am I!' I wailed at the floor. The floor didn't comment. The boards were impervious to my woe. Some people are stoic in the face of disaster gazing calmly as their worlds collapse with a detached sangfroid. I'm not one of them. I ride life's emotional waves on a transparent lambskin surfboard plunging from invincible to drowning in seconds. The only good news is that I rise up just as fast. Onlookers have little choice but to ride out the lows and hang in there for the next chug up hill.

Adnan's forehead rumpled in bemusement. He stood up thoughtfully and bent to throw a log on the wood burner. He sat back and we both watched the fingers of flame reach out of the aperture in the front as if trying to escape the metal furnace they were writhing within. The heat warmed our knees and our faces, but our backs were freezing. That's what you get when you build walls with concrete and no insulation. But hey, at least Adnan *had* walls. Mine were going to be cocoa powder by the end of the week. Adnan lit a cigarette. I poached one from him. As I inhaled and exhaled, the cold layer of foreboding coating my intestines dissipated slightly.

'There's got to be *something* we can do,' murmured Adnan carefully.

'What? *What*? We can't change the weather! All we can do is hope and pray that somehow the bags don't freeze right through.'

'They probably won't. I mean, one or two degrees under is the lowest temperature. It might only go down to that for a few minutes,' Adnan reasoned. I pouted. Probably and praying weren't good enough in my book. I suddenly realised I needed a plan, a proper plan.

'I think I'm going to cancel the work tomorrow. It'll be too cold. It's going to be four degrees at five am according to this. Can you imagine working with wet mud in that?'

Adnan pulled his mouth into a sympathetic line. I yanked my phone from its charger and began pressing the numbers until Celal answered.

'Aye?' Celal's voice was always reassuring. I breathed.

'Celal, it's going to be really cold tomorrow. Perhaps we should give work a miss?'

'Yup. Weather's takin' a turn, we're in for a right butt-freezin', that we are. I'm just 'appy I don't have a greenhouse cos those poor buggers are gonna be up all night lighting stoves to keep them tomatoes from freezing.'

I could always count on Celal for the village news. He was a long, healthy, leaf-covered branch of the Yapraklı grapevine. I said goodbye and threw the phone onto the table in a huff.

'What did he say?' Adnan eyed the phone and my temper dubiously.

'Poor bastards with greenhouses are lighting stoves. It's definitely going below zero.'

'Lighting stoves? What, in the polytunnels?'

'Yes.'

Adnan's face became animated. 'Hey, we could do that! We can make a fire inside. That will stop it freezing for sure. Genius!'

'You think so?'

'Sure! We just need something to light it in, you know an old tin drum or something.'

'Like those big oil drums Celal brought round to use as scaffolding.'

'They're for scaffolding? How's that gonna work?'

'Oh I dunno. He's got some idea about laying a plank on them I think. Anyway, I suppose we could light a fire in one of them.'

'You bet!' Adnan raised his hand to high-five me. I grinned and missed his hand completely because I'm not from North America, nor a teenage rapper, and therefore don't really understand the mechanics of high-fives. I went for a second hand slap, and managed to make contact.

'Way to go sista!' cheered Adnan.

'Woo hoo! We have a plan, and it's a good one. Ha ha!' I was cruising up the back of a new wave, knees braced, arms outstretched. I could feel the swell under my feet and the breeze in my hair. I had a plan. It was a bit rough round the edges and sported a few coffee stains, but it was something.

***

The next day, I was up at the crack of dawn. Adnan's house was truly Siberian, and I woke feeling a chill across the top of my head. I sat up. There was a movement outside the window, something slipped across it; a giant feather, or was it a bird? I blinked and peered out. The black muzzle of Apo grinned back at me in all its Anatolian faithfulness. He must have followed us the previous night without my realising. I loved Apo, and saw him as a fine omen. Apo had a habit of turning up when you were afraid, or in a fix. He would wander over, rump swaying, huge Kangal balls swinging, looking quite the mythical guardian, and being almost the size of a lion it made one feel protected to have him around.

I dressed, stuffed my feet in my wellies and quietly slipped out of the house. I started the car. Apo ran behind it, fur-covered muscles rippling, great paws galloping over the mud.

I spent the morning collecting pieces of wood from the forest next door. Hauling it back to my land, I chainsawed it down to size. It was cold even at midday, and I pulled my hat over my aching ears. After lunch a nearby friend phoned. I happened to mention the minus one freezing earthbag disaster looming.

'Oh Kerry, you don't need to stay up all night. Just cover the north side wall with plastic to keep the wind off and you'll be fine. It won't freeze.'

'Really?'

'Yes. I've done it with flower beds. It's enough. We're not living in Canada.'

I spent the afternoon mulling it over. It was a risk the greenhouse owners weren't taking, so should I? Yet, the thought of staying awake the entire night to man a fire was less than inspiring. I trod this way and that, feeling the walls (obviously still wet), sniffing the air, talking to the trees. But in the end laziness won. Pulling a sheet of plastic from behind the shed, I hammered it to the wooden strip anchors we were inserting into the door and window frames. Once the north side was covered, I mooched over to my tent. It was now mid-afternoon and a pale winter sun had turned the canvas silver. The wind was biting. I opened the door and peered inside my home; mattress in the corner, toiletries packed in a plastic fruit crate, a small suitcase that acted as my wardrobe, books, bag of toiletries. This was my life. It was the only tiny square of protection I had against the elements. In summer it had seemed ample, even luxurious, but from this new cold winter perspective it looked paltry and cramped. I wondered what it was going to be like in there that night, my first night below zero. If you are properly equipped, zero degrees is a picnic. There are mountaineers who have to dig their tents out of snowdrifts in the morning. But a $50 Carrefour tent and a ten-year-old winter sleeping bag bought on the cheap from Jacks in Colchester doesn't constitute 'properly equipped'. I pulled the sleeping bag toward me and searched the label by the zip. Between 5 and 15 degrees was its claim. I would need plenty of layers.

I zipped up the tent door and wandered to my kitchen. Putting the kettle on the hob, I laid in the hammock swinging under Grandmother Olive. I closed my eyes and let nature's rhythm touch me; the cool air on my cheeks, the soft whoosh of the tree tops, the quiet scuttling of beetles, the smell of bark, earth and oxygen, the faint croak of frogs, and the chatter of small birds. In minutes my anxiety evaporated. As the hammock swung left and right, I felt my head clear and my body relax. My land was doing it again. She was taking care of me. I could almost sense Gaia stroking my forehead. I opened my eyes. Then I sighed. *Take care of the house. I don't know how, but just take care of it.* Releasing my grip, I let the anchor of responsible decision-making go.

I was pulled from my reverie by a vibrating in my pocket. My phone. I pulled it out and pressed the green phone button.

'Hey there neighbour!' It was Adnan. 'I'm assuming you're staying here tonight.' How wondrously pleasing those words were to my chilled ear.

I made a feeble and frankly insincere attempt to refuse his kind offer a) because I didn't want to bother him and b) because I like to be independent. Then I caved quite pathetically. 'Well, if you're sure you don't mind.'

'Stay here as long as you want. My *God*! You can't sleep out there in this weather. Just sleep over till you've finished the house. No worries on my part. That's what friends are for!'

Sadly, friendship is far too underrated these days. People are obsessed with romantic couplings, nuclear families and their children, and I'm not saying these don't have a place. Yet from my perspective, that of a voluntarily single marginal, the friendship horn needs a good toot too. I'm indebted to my friends; pals who have accepted my quirks, who have opened their homes to me when times have got tough, who have shared my interests, who have survived the test of time, who have saved my risk-taking butt. Friends can let you be and love you simultaneously. Compared to the majority of lovers, they are less suffocating, less demanding and altogether more pleasant to be around most of the time, and despite my hyper independence and contrariness, I am blessed with plenty of them.

Stumbling from my hammock, I stepped into the kitchen. The kettle was pumping steam out and gurgling happily. I grabbed a teabag and threw it into a mug with the hot water. Walking to the centre of my land, I raised my mug to the view. 'Here's to friendship,' I whispered to the mountains. Their rocky heads jutted all about me in a haphazard semi-circle, faces greenly hirsute.

Soon, the dog of darkness licked up the last drops of daylight from the plate of the sky. I boarded the donkey-buzzard. I sped up the hill, the car squeaking and rattling over the craters and rocks. Then I swerved down the other side of the mountain, round bends and twists, through the clutter of houses that is Yapraklı village, past the brook with the collapsed boulders cluttering the roadside, and through the blackened pine forests that lead into the valley. Gnarled trunks stricken yellow by my headlights lurched and leered before they flicked out of view. Wild eyes shone out at me every now and again; either feline or canine or even boarish. Not a human was to be seen. Eventually, I arrived.

There, on the corner of the river at the entrance to the valley was my nearest corner shop. It was run by a short, grumpy, religious right-winger who happily saw no contradiction in stocking alcohol, condoms and extra-long cigarette papers, no doubt because the majority of his customers included irreligious epicureans from Istanbul, *yabancı* and a sizeable amount of alcoholic locals. You can always count on capitalism to crack a zealot.

I bought a bottle of whisky and a bag full of snacks, before driving round and up and down and round all the way back to Adnan's house on the hill. When I stepped out of the car I was almost knocked breathless by the chill and the clarity of the night sky. The asteroid belt was as clear and sparkling as a freshly sown furrow of fairy dust.

That night Adnan and I sat by a ravenous stove, cheeks burning, backs freezing, and got unashamedly hammered. We babbled all night as the temperature plummeted, eventually falling into slurring confessions regarding all manner of past demeanours and family histories that shall never be voiced again, not least because I can't quite remember them. Finally, I staggered into the icebox spare room and collapsed fully dressed under two thick duvets. I sank into a furry state of inebriated unconsciousness as a layer of frost crept over the outside sills. The Mediterranean was freezing for the first time since I'd set foot on it 15 years ago.

***

There is an argument that the way we view reality actually changes reality; the window through which we look at the world is not just a gaping hole in the wall between inside and out, but some sort of atom-shifting portal. Positive thinking apostles, new-agers and self-help gurus tend to rally behind this attitude. And then there is another argument which states this is mystical hogwash. Reality hasn't changed at all, instead our awareness is selective. There is one reality and we are seeing it differently (namely the way we want to). Staunch rationalists and anyone else whose job is dependent on appearing cleverly sceptical tend to uphold this view. Which, if either of these two explanations, my experience with my land is summed up by, I leave you to decide. All I can say is, I stepped onto my land holding a fairly irrational belief that it was going to look after me, and it was the window through which I viewed everything that happened there after. Did this outlook affect my land in any way? Or was it just that I was looking for positive feedback?

'Oh fuck!'

I drove through Adnan's normally muddy track, only instead of wheels churning mud, they were bouncing over hardened ridges. I gulped at the fine layer of white that still peppered anything out of the sun's reach. It was hardly a deep freeze. Those from colder climbs would have snorted at my agitation. But for me it was unusual. I searched through the vaults of my memory. Had I ever seen frost here before?

Within minutes I arrived at my land. Apo the dog hadn't followed me, and as the lump in my throat climbed higher I missed his loping gait and his massive hound presence. Pushing the car door to, I walked past the tower of hydraulic lime bags that line the entrance to my property, through the leafless wild dog roses and the shrivelled oregano, until I reached the earthbag building site. The ground was hard underfoot, semi petrified. It was about 7:30 am.

As I approached the house, I scanned the land for signs of freezing. It was at that exact moment, the sun hauled itself over the pines on the south-east side. The slope suddenly turned bright green, grass tips gleaming with dew. This meant there was no frost at the front of the house. I walked over to a basil plant I'd cultivated throughout the summer. It was still alive, green leaves bending to the sun as if nothing had happened. I wandered about the house and felt the bags. They were cold and damp, and not in any way frozen.

'It's a miracle,' I whispered.

And it was. Over the course of the next couple of days as the temperature dropped further, news of other people's losses filtered over to me. Down in the valley, the damage was palpable. Puddles had iced over. The cacti, succulents and banana plants were all frozen to the quick and hung in withered brown heaps. Anyone with vegetables outside a heated greenhouse lost their crop. In Alakir, children blinked at the dusting of white and ran about excitedly screaming 'snow!'. Yet I had been spared. How? As usual, it was my land that had saved me. Unbeknown to me at the time, my property was in fact occupying a tiny micro-climate. The plot slopes to the south, which means it gets a good eight hours of sun even on the shortest day of the year, and is protected on the north by a steep forested hill. Those icy north winds hardly touch it. My plot of land and the one below me remain about two degrees warmer than our neighbours and up to five degrees warmer than five km away in the valley. Celal and Dudu, though next door to me, were by no means as lucky as the north wind whipped their beans and killed off the last of their summer vegetables.

I exhaled slowly, relishing the feeling of the warm breath as it left my lips. Then I wandered down the hill a little, and sat on the ground. I wanted to speak to my land, to thank it. I ran my fingers through its green hair, and patted and kissed its earth hide. It smelt sweet and sensuous like coffee liquor. It smelt of life, and of mysteries I knew nothing about. I shivered. And then I laughed and laughed and laughed.

'Woo hoo!' I stretched out on my back and rolled down the slope like I had when I was about seven years old on the primary school slope in Wivenhoe. 'My land is the best place on Earth!' I crowed. And it was. It still is. Long may it remain so.

For a brief interlude of two or three days, I had the time to gather my head, my heart and my body. During the building mania of the past weeks, these three elements of my being had become somewhat out of sync. My head was bombing through ideas at a dizzying rate, my body was crawling in exhaustion, and my heart had got lost somewhere between the two. As I once more became a single functioning entity, I remembered all was well, life was on my side, my land loved me and I was safe.

That afternoon, I called the various members of the earthbag team and informed them we'd restart work the next day. It all seemed to be snapping in to place.

Warped Frames

'Erm, Kerry, have you noticed? The windows have warped.' Esra was standing in front of the south-west facing window, scrutinising the frames.

Celal and Ahmet immediately downed tools. I sighed. There was always *something*, wasn't there? My initial reaction to any given problem noticed by the team was to brush it off as not serious, because nine times out of ten, it wasn't. In fact, half the time I suspected it was the labourer's answer to filibustering. We could easily waste half-an-hour doing nothing when a problem arose.

Stepping round to the window, empty orange sack still in hand, I studied the top and the bottom. I could have pulled out a tape measure to check, but what was the point? It was plain to a myopic absinthe drinker that the window frames had buckled. I dropped the sack.

Initially, when disaster strikes, as it so often does, one copes by praying or hoping that the trouble is limited to a small area. I scampered round to the other side of the house to check on the other window. Now, my heart didn't literally drop a centimetre because that would have been medically fatal, but there was certainly a heavy slump in my chest area. Instead of sitting square, both windows had collapsed into trapezoids. I bit my lip.

The sun was directly over us, the shadows no more than tiny slivers of darkness. It cruised in and out of globules of cloud like a golden Titanic through icebergs. Wincing a little, I stepped over to the front door. It was the widest aperture in the building, so it boded badly. My chin hit my chest. Not only had it turned into a parallelogram, but it was leaning forwards as well. The pressure of the bags (which is not inconsiderable as tons of earth are compressed on each row) had forced every one of the frames, turning them into giant versions of a primary school pupil's geometry set.

The team were standing at the front of the house, waiting for the verdict. I turned from the doorframe to see six eyes resting expectantly on me.

'OK, we screwed up.'

'Now there's a surprise,' quipped Ahmet. 'We need the *mudur*, we do. He'd know what to do.'

I shot him a radium-tipped barb of a look.

'Ahem, so do we carry on bagging, or what?'

'No, we're going to fix the windows.'

'How?' Esra pushed a chestnut strand of hair out of her face, and slid it behind her ear.

'By doing what we should have done in the beginning and wedging braces in there.'

'And where'll we be gettin' these braces at this time on a freeze-your-arse-off winter's day?' said Celal rather

145

unhelpfully. He had a giant woolly hat pulled over his ears like a tea cosy and had taken up his trademark position of spade-leaning.

'We'll make them of course! Oh stop being so negative for God's sake! It's not *that* hard, is it?' I huffed over to the wood store, which was basically all my wood wrapped in a large sheet of plastic on the ground. I pulled out a couple of floorboards and threw them in Ahmet's direction. Then I grabbed the tape measure and re-measured how wide the frames should have been. My three paid helpers stood round in a circle and gawked. After I'd drawn pencil lines on the wood, Ahmet sawed them to size. Then Esra and I jammed them into each frame, which is far easier to type on a screen than manage in real life. It took the best part of the afternoon.

As the sun began its daily pilgrimage toward the horizon, I stood back and eyed the frames. They were fairly straight, and seemed to be holding...for now. It was perhaps for the best that Adnan had taken a day off to write an article. I calculated if we worked fast enough, the next morning we'd have the window height filled with earthbags before he arrived, and then it would be too late to do anything else about them. Just why I had adopted this ludicrously self-defeating attitude of bodging my own house and viewed Adnan's well-intentioned precision as something I should controvert stems from a congenital propensity I have to rebel against any kind of authority. Traffic lights, diets, straight lines, governments, precise measurements; within the dark recesses of my subconscious, they are all related parts of a secret conspiracy of control the outside world is trying to foist upon me.

'See you tomorrow then,' waved Esra. Celal and Ahmet murmured their goodbyes, and off the troupe stomped to board their donkey-buzzard. I was left to sit on a rock and watch the last remnants of light drain from the view. The far off lamps of Alakir pricked orange through the dusk. One by one the mountains disappeared into the grey.

There was one thing that *was* going in the right direction; the temperature. It had grown significantly warmer over the past two days. I decided to sleep in my tent again. Strange as it may seem, I missed it; the sound of the night animals, the rustling of the wind on the canvas, the first silvery strands of morning to slide over the tent, the chatter of the early birds. Contrary to what one might think, once I lived in a world without walls, rather than feeling permanently vulnerable, instead I felt connected and safe. Was this based on an exchange between me and my environment? Or was it a psychological survival tactic I'd learned to stop me dissolving into a jittering wreck each night. Again, that depends on just which way your windows are buckling.

***

The next day I awoke to find the sky had dropped all the way into the valley, at least that's how it looked from my tent portal. The usually wide open vault above the mountains had been subsumed into a mass of thick cloud. The stratus wasn't black and ominous, more grey and grumpy. I climbed out of my tent, stuck my feet into my wellies and trudged over to my 'bathroom'. It consisted of the wooden box of a composting toilet wedged into some bushes, a water canister set on some rocks with a hose pipe attached, and a patch of small stones to create a mud-free flooring. I washed and brushed my teeth. I sat on my throne and watched the birds flutter overhead. Then I headed for the 'kitchen' to make some coffee.

The Aksoy team arrived bang on eight. I marvelled at Esra and Ahmet's time-keeping, because it was a rarity in rural Turkey. Within ten minutes we were earthbagging again, moving brick by wet earth brick round and round the layers. The pace had decelerated for a number of reasons; first, it was fiddly now that we had windows to fit around, and second the higher we rose, the more difficult it was to lift the bags. Celal's scaffolding had come into play by this point, and Esra and I were tottering on a plank balanced upon two rusty oil drums. From this wobbly perch we set the bags on the barbed wire. Celal was at his usual station and shovelling earth. Ahmet was making sure the correct number of yoghurt pots of dirt went into the bag and subsequently lifting it onto the plank. This isn't what the earthbag bible recommends, nor the *Natural Building Blog*. What one is *supposed* to do is fill the bag on the wall to prevent a potential back injury. The trouble was, the progress was more sluggish this way, and the process left Ahmet huffing, sighing and rolling those blue ocular marbles of his in impatience. He seemed to prefer the jeopardy of a hernia to the slow agony of watching us pour earth, pot by pot, into the sack.

'Ahoy there!' A voice came from on high. I squeaked in terror. It was Adnan. He stood under a great pine just above the land with his rucksack on, scanning the terrain. He was wearing a black T-shirt, and from my distance looked a bit like a large, bipedal ant.

'Oh shit! He's going to make us redo the front door!' I squawked in Turkish to the Aksoy team. And then brightly, 'Hello there, neighbour. You're nice and early!' to Adnan.

'Yeah, too much in my head. I could do with some manual labour to bring me back down to Earth.'

'*Mudur!*' Ahmet yelled, 'You wanna take a look at the door.' He said it in Turkish, but Adnan caught the familiar word *kapı*.

'Door? Everything alright there with the front door?'

I sighed. I'd been busted.

Adnan trotted onto the land, chin up, eyes sweeping the site for trouble. Whether he'd chosen his T-shirt by design or not, I have no idea. It was black with 'I'LL BE THERE' emblazoned in white across the back. As it turned out, that was going to be somewhat prophetic. Circling the earthbag site, he studied each frame. Then, to my horror, he nipped into the shed and came out with the spirit level. I was doomed, but pretended otherwise. We carried on our earthbagging as though nothing was happening. Ahmet deposited a heavy eight-pot bag onto our plank, shaking our footings so that Esra and I had to hang on to the wall. On a one-two-three, we both then heaved the bag up to waist height, and onto the plywood runner. We positioned it, pulled out the runner and then whacked the bag into place. After two bags had been felled, I was starting to wonder why I wasn't hearing anything from Adnan. I stole a glance over in his direction. He was standing, spirit level in hand, frowning at the front door. Esra and I exchanged flinching looks and waited silently for the boot to fall.

Adnan raised his head. 'So we should have made boxes, eh?'

I nodded meekly. 'But there was a picture of a door frame made like ours, remember?'

'Yeah, I guess we should have braced it better, right?'

'And used thicker wood,' I added.

'Sure. But hey, maybe you can do something *creative* with these tapering window frames, like some awesome shapes that no one else has for a window.'

'What do you mean tapering windows? We straightened them out yesterday!' I knew the door was going to be an issue, but the windows?

'Well they sure ain't straight now, Kerry.'

I rested my head briefly on the earthbag wall and quietly uttered some coarse language to the polypropylene. Then I hopped down from the plank and surveyed the damage. Sure enough, the windows were almost back to the same trapezoid shape they had been the day before. The wedges had slipped, or popped out, or were simply incapable of holding off the increasing pressure as we tamped round the rising layers of earthbags.

'Oh for fuck's sake!' I kicked the wall, then threw my gardening gloves on the ground. 'Are they leaning out again, as well?'

'Ah, now I hadn't gotten round to checking that yet,' said Adnan waving the spirit level about like a dowser's rod. Then, taking stock of the direction my mood was sliding, he rested his chin thoughtfully on the metal oblong and said nothing more. I stomped over to the 'kitchen' to put the kettle on. Celal raised his head hopefully.

'Ah! Good glass o' *çay*, that's what we need innit? Praps you can get the carpenter up 'ere to sort it all out.'

While I sulked in the kitchen, Esra and Ahmet made themselves look busy by rattling yoghurt pots and moving the bag stand to and fro. Celal followed Adnan round the house to survey the window frame debacle for himself. As the kettle began to hiss, a strange wind picked up. It rattled the pines overhead. I looked up briefly to see Adnan, once again standing on the raised parapet of earth behind the house, scratching his head. He saw me and blinked.

'Kerry, now don't get mad, but I feel I have to tell you. The walls...they're not curving round anymore. They're going straight.'

I was holding a jar of teabags in one hand and a jar of sugar in the other. I must have looked about as forlorn as an earthbagger can.

'So what you're saying is my roundhouse has turned into a frigging pentagon.'

Adnan moved his lips wordlessly while his head waved ambivalently from side to side. 'Hey, pentagons are cool too. I mean not as cool as circles obviously...'

I stalked over to our little wooden table and slammed down the jars. Then I turned around. I might even have put my hands on my hips, which is embarrassing.

'The CIA has a pentagon. Satanists use pentagons. Pentagons are not fucking cool! They're pointy and angular and made of five straight lines. You know what Hundertwasser said? Straight lines are the devil's work. And they're probably something to do with the Illuminati, as well!' I roared. People were listening to my rant all the way down in the valley.

'Erm actually Satanists have penta*grams*, but I hear what you're saying.'

'Well, I'm not having a penta anything, nor a quadra anything, nor a flipping do-deca anything. This is going to be a circle; a big fuckoff cornerless ring of Mother Earth.' I turned to the Turkish trio who were edging hesitantly towards the tea table. I pointed my finger to the sky and stabbed the air emphatically. 'And once we've drunk tea we're going to take off those offending bags and round those straight lines!' I shouted in Turkish. 'Pentagon? Hmph. Over my dead body!'

It was one of those days, and the only positive thing about having 'one of those days' is that they finally come to an end and a new, altogether better day dawns. Sometimes, though, that seems to take rather a long time. The team sat uncomfortably around the table and sipped their tea. Ahmet sloped off for a peaceful cigarette and Adnan joined him. I fumed silently on a rock, staring at the front of the house where the main thrust of the trouble was. The gap between the front door and the windows was relatively small which had led to difficulties in creating enough of a curve as we laid the bags between them. I saw quite clearly that Adnan was right, and the front walls were flattening. Meanwhile the door and window frames were all over the place. It looked such a mess, so far from the vision of a perfect circle I had in my head, and I was wholeheartedly discouraged. I wanted it to be immaculate. Yet, as with everything in the real world, it wasn't.

And that is so often how we see it, isn't it? That the image in our head is the perfection, and its physical counterpart more or less flawed. It might be the 21st century but I had nonetheless made myself unconsciously comfy in Plato's cave of ideas. I was falling into the trap of considering the world of imagined ideas pristine, while I viewed the physical world as a marred reflection of it. It's those plans again. Those mental images we humans so love to pin over reality.

Sighing, I stood up and walked to the gap in the front of the house which was to be the front door. I stepped over the threshold and trod on the plastic covered floorboards until I was standing in the centre of the house. I turned. I looked out from the warped frames of both the front door and the two adjacent windows. I noticed the front door was leaning to the right like a rectangular, pinewood drunk.

I closed my eyes. Then opened them again. This time, instead of gaping at those godforsaken frames, I now stared at the view beyond. The mountains were a jumble of geological humps rising on either side. The forest in front was an overgrown mishmash of pine limbs, none of which rose in neat pyramid shapes like those on Christmas cards. Instead they twisted and curled and arced, sometimes they jutted at odd angles, sometimes they were broken and leaning on their neighbours, sometimes the branches had become entangled. Spiky bushes pushed through here and there wherever they found a patch of unclaimed sunlight. There were clumps and craters, landslides and fallen rocks. Nothing did what it was told. It was a mess.

While my body remained in the centre of the earth circle, my mind drifted out of the leaning door frame and met the world outside. It was untamed, raw and intoxicatingly beautiful. It was alive and oozing magic. Granite clouds hobbled over the hills like angry old men. The mountains had turned dark emerald. I inhaled a different kind of perfection; not the remote and marginally sterile perfection of the mind, but the rampant perfection of the Earth.

After a few moments, I stepped back outside. This time when I looked at the frames, I saw something else. This was a human house, an earth house, not a box to be approved by city-planners nor some product issued from a machine. It was a natural house, and that meant it wasn't going to adhere to ideas of perfection, nor follow blindly some image in my head. It was going to be whatever it was going to be.

I turned to the crew – who had left their empty teacups on the table and were now loitering by the front of the house – now somewhat calmed down.

'Scrap what I said about taking all the bags off. We'll just adjust the last layer and try and get rounder on the next layers up.' Then I repeated this word for word in Turkish. There was a visible sigh of relief from Esra. Celal shrugged. Ahmet picked up the bag stand and began folding a new sack over the edges ready to fill.

'As for the frames, Adnan, see if you can find a way to keep them from buckling any more. And somehow we need to push the door frame back into position or I fear it's going to pop right out.'

'I hear ya. I'm on it,' said Adnan with gusto. 'Ah that's what I like about you, Kerry. In the face of disaster, you've always got another plan.'

I wrinkled my forehead at that. Interesting. I saw myself as highly *un*planned, but from Adnan's perspective I was a master goal designer. I took stock of the sky again. It was sullen and heavy like a pre-menstrual belly.

'Another thing. Before we go tonight, let's cover this thing in a tarp,' I added. 'I've got a bad feeling about the weather and those virgin juniper boards are sitting ducks right now. If it does rain, heaven forbid, then this thing will fill up like a swimming pool.' I pointed at the earthbag ring, which did indeed resemble a giant orange paddling pool. There were nods all around.

Evening came for us, as it always did, and everyone was happy to see it. Adnan and I had wedged new planks in the frames, we were up another layer of earthbags, and this time they were curving. We had pulled a spanking new sheet of plastic over the entire house and hoisted it up in the centre using a pole. The edges of the sheet reached over the walls and were fixed on the ground by large rocks. It created the impression of a giant, white tent. I had half a mind to sleep in there, but in the end I couldn't be bothered to move my mattress. In retrospect that was exceedingly fortunate.

The light vacated my land along with my earthbag team. I waved as the Aksoys drove away feeling warmly disposed to them all, sort of an earthbag shepherdess with her flock. Even so, we were tired. It was time for a day off. I drove Adnan up the hill and dropped him at the track to his house. I watched him amble down the road to home. I grinned as 'I'LL BE THERE' disappeared into the dusk.

***

Less than an hour later, I was snuggled into my sleeping bag relishing the sudden mildness of the weather. I didn't even need my hat on. Propping myself on a heap of pillows, I pulled out the earthbag bible. We had almost reached the top of the windows, so lintels were coming next. Chris in

Fethiye had advised me that square windows with lintels were far easier than trying to make an arch, and I was all for easy at that juncture. We were also about to insert three tiny porthole type windows at the back of the house, and a stove pipe opening as well. I scratched my head as I considered these details and wondered about the litter of issues they'd doubtless spawn. It always looked so straightforward in the book. Everything slotted neatly into place. Nothing buckled. Nothing sloped. Nothing collapsed.

I looked up through my tent door and mourned the lack of stars. They had become my reference points since I slept outside. When both they and the lights from Alakir disappeared, it felt as though my tent had come free of its moorings and was adrift in an ocean of dark uncertainty. I zipped down the hatch for the night and wriggled into my sleeping bag. Exhaustion sank onto me like a heavy and slightly musty old blanket. It was then that I heard it.

Tap tap tap. It was a light pattering on the canvas. Rain. My stomach lurched. Groaning aloud, I sat up. Pulling out my laptop, I turned it on and inserted the dongle in its side. I had to see what the weather oracles were predicting. No wind was audible at that stage, just an amiable drumming of raindrops. It sounded innocuous, but would it deteriorate? I thought about my juniper floor and kicked myself for the umpteenth time. Opening up the browser tab for the local weather, I let the hourly forecast load. I swallowed slowly as the report was revealed. Rain until midnight. Then heavy rain. Then downpour. I was so tired, emotionally, mentally and physically, I just couldn't see how I was going to cope with a deluge. But what I thought about it didn't really matter. The sky wasn't taking me into account.

I was pulled in two directions. Fatigue was telling me to forget about it, lie down, leave the floor to its fate and hope for the best. Worry, mean-spirited tormenter that it is, was having none of it. It stabbed through the eiderdown of my weariness needling me with any number of alarming comments. *Have you secured the plastic well enough? Could you cover the floor any better? Is it raining harder yet? Perhaps you should tie the plastic. Perhaps you should sit up and watch.* In truth, there was nothing of any practical value that I could do, but worry didn't care. It had a hold on my adrenalin and was stressing me out.

Reluctantly and slightly hopelessly, I submitted to my whining mind. I slid out of my sleeping bag. Opening the front hatch, I stuck my legs out. I found my wellies, grabbed my torch and made for the earthbag house. Flicking the beam over the plastic sheeting, I tried to assess if it would hold or not. I came to the conclusion that a light rain would be harmless, but a downpour would be pretty fatal. Yet what could I do? The answer was not a lot, thus I returned to my foam mattress bed and tried my best to get some shuteye.

It was a fitful night of anxious tossings and turnings, of subconsciously pricked ears, of the odd sitting bolt upright and hurriedly yanking apart the zipper to check outside. This restlessness continued until two in the morning (I know because I was obsessively checking the clock). It was then the belly of darkness finally split and let its watery contents descend. The patter turned into a heavy hammering as the rain slid off the sides of the tent. There was, however, no wind. And that was why, at the very least, my tent remained dry. But what about the other tent? The one we'd hastily tacked up over the house?

The downpour lasted a good hour before it paused, or at the very least slowed to a reasonable rate. Heart racing, I fumbled for my torch and located my umbrella. My wellies, which were just below the platform, had filled with water. I emptied them into the mud before sticking my feet inside. Wet wellies was just one of my many physical miseries, and I paid my cold feet little attention. With a sense of morbid trepidation, I squelched over to the house once again. My torchlight skipped over the plastic sheeting. The rocks were still in place. I moved the beam of light up to the where the pole in the middle should have been.

On seeing what had happened, I gulped. Panic began bubbling in my chest and throat. It was now three in the morning, a time of night when even under the most benign circumstances one can feel assailed by anxiety attacks, when insignificant concerns swell into cataclysms. This wasn't a particularly benign circumstance. The pole that was holding up the sheeting had fallen down, and in the centre of the house, the plastic had inverted and filled up to become an enormous bowl of water. I entered the house by the back door and gaped. The sheeting was bowed and in places actually touched the floor. So far though, the floor was still dry. But as soon as more rain fell, or the rocks gave up the ghost, the plastic would collapse. And then...

Resting the torch on one of the shelf supports that we'd previously slotted into the wall, I gingerly picked my way about the concave tarp. Grabbing any stick of wood I could lay my hands on, I had a bash at pushing up the plastic. It was too heavy. Every move I made threatened to dislodge the rocks outside and weaken what was currently a very precarious structure. It wasn't a one person job. Someone needed to be outside holding on to the edge of plastic, while another pushed up from the inside.

Taking a few deep breaths I checked the time on my phone; 3:12 am. Honestly, who can you possibly call at that time on a rainy night? 'I'LL BE THERE' flashed into my mind the way only a T-shirt slogan can. I remembered Adnan saying I could call anytime day or night in an emergency, but had he been being polite? Of course he had! Of course he didn't want me to call him and wrench him out of bed. What can I say? I was desperate.

161

I stepped outside the house again and walked around the edge with the torch, surveying for further trouble. It was then that a light wind picked up. The tarp rustled. I groaned as the rain began to spatter down once more with what seemed deliberate tenacity. Pulling my phone out, I talked pleadingly to the floor, 'Adnan brother, I'm so sorry for what I'm about to do, and if you don't pick up I will completely forgive you. In fact, if I were you, I wouldn't pick up. I'd roll over and go back to sleep.' Then I took a deep breath and pressed the green call button. Ring. Ring. Ring. Ring. Ring.

'Urgh, flum, brum, agh urgh hello?'

'Adnan, I'm so, so sorry to call you at this time, I apologise I really do...' I grovelled in this rather unattractive manner until Adnan grew impatient.

'What's up?'

So I told him all about the slipped pole, and the giant water-filled plastic fishbowl hanging over the juniper floor, and the rain which was getting worse.

'OK. Give me a minute. I'm on my way,' he said, with hardly more effort than if it had been three in the afternoon and I'd invited him round for coffee. I leaned my back on the shed door and enjoyed a long exhalation as the relief spread from head to toe. I wasn't alone. Suddenly everything seemed salvageable. Realising I was now sliding into massive friendship favour debt, I made a mental note to buy Adnan a large bottle of whisky at the next opportunity.

The rain continued to splash down. I waited restlessly, pacing round and round the house. I waited about twenty minutes, and then a surprisingly lively Adnan appeared. It must have been a brisk walk.

'Hey there!'

'Adnan, what can I say? You're a star.'

He galloped onto the plot, hair shining wet. I shone the torch while Adnan wandered about and surveyed the damage. Soon, he came up with the far more sensible idea of scooping the water out before attempting to raise the tarp. He held the edges, while I grabbed a large paint container, and pot by pot began the not insignificant job of draining the pool from the lower parts of the plastic. After a good ten minutes of scoop and slosh, the lake began to decrease in size. At this point I grabbed the offending fallen pole and began to slowly raise the plastic, just as I'd seen stall owners at the local bazaar do on rainy days. And just as in the Sunday bazaar, the water that had collected in the dips glided in passerby-soaking cascades onto the ground outside the house.

'Agh! Thanks! Wet sneakers, just what I've always wanted.'

'Sorry, Adnan. You can start making a list when you get back – *Ways Kerry put me through hell.*'

'Ah, what are friends for?' Adnan was cheerfully lifting the plastic over his head.

'Erm, dragging out of bed at three am and soaking from head to toe, apparently.' I shook my head in wonder at the guy. This scenario seemed a pretty good reason for homicide, if you asked me.

Eventually, we managed to rid the plastic of every last drop of water. Then, determined souls that we were, we re-erected the tent with the pole in the centre of the floor (which was still covered in another layer of plastic and had thus miraculously survived with all but the tiniest of puddles). I tried to render the pole a little less prone to the elements by jamming it between a wooden chair and the paint pot filled with rocks. We dragged the plastic over the outside of the house again and secured it with rocks on the ground. It was spitting now, and I could feel the ache of sleeplessness in my bones. I checked my phone for the time: it was now five am. I leaned against the shed.

'I'm done. It's enough. Whatever will be will be, from here on in,' I said.

Adnan nodded. 'I think it's going to be fine. So glad we saved that floor. That would have been a real shame.'

'I can't even drive you up the hill. The car won't make it up that slope. Tell you what, I'll walk you up instead.' I felt I had to do something for the man, even if it was only a little self-flagellation.

'Ah let's go back to mine, get dry and have a coffee, eh?'

I sighed. 'Sounds great.'

And off we plodded, two damp, tired but nonetheless successful souls, up the mud slick track to the house on the hill.

Barbed Wire Belle

By the luck of the gods, that one night of rain was all Father Sky had in store for us. The next few days opened their stalls with sunshine and the blithesome chirping of birds. It was now week four of the building process. We were three days into December. I was pushing the limits of my luck as by mid-December the Mediterranean is on the doorstep of its winter of hurricanes, floods and other biblical style weather catastrophes. On top of that, my money was running out. I had about $3500 left and the roof was going to eat into most of that. An unsettling thought had begun to gnaw at the floorboards in the back rooms of my mind. What was going to happen when the money finally trickled away? I had no income. If the house was finished, I'd survive. But if not? I think at that point, I was still reasonably confident I'd be living in my mud home in a week or two. I wonder what I'd have done if I'd known the terrible truth.

It was afternoon. Esra, Ahmet, Celal and I were assembled by Grandmother Olive. A massive wooden slab lay in front of us. It was about three metres long, 30 centimetres wide and 20 centimetres deep. We all stared at it speculatively. We'd arrived at the lintels.

Ahmet bent down, slid his hands under the beam and lifted it to test the weight. He let it drop back down with a thud. 'I'll get up on the wall and Dad can pass it up,' he said. I shrugged. It seemed simple enough. Inside I was fretting, though. We'd just spent two days on the small portal windows at the back of the house. I'd erroneously used 10-by-10s as lintels. We'd laid one layer of earthbags over them, after which Ahmet had walked round the wall pounding each bag with the marble bird bath. When he reached the portal windows, we heard three consecutive cracks. The lintels had failed.

The next day, I drove to the wood yard and bought three monstrous 30-by-20 wooden bricks. We fixed them above the portal windows and replaced the bags over the top. They survived a tamping. But how would it be with a larger opening, such as my two-metre-wide door?

Ahmet was now crouched on the earthbag wall by the west-facing window. Celal stooped, picked up one end of the lintel and dragged it to his son's position on the wall. Ahmet reached down and grabbed the end. Celal ran to the back of the beam and lifted it. Within minutes it was sitting squarely above my window, looking reassuringly solid.

'There you go! I'm gonna walk on it to check it holds.'

'Ahmet! That's not really the safest way to test it,' I wagged my finger at him.

Too late, he was standing in the middle of the beam grinning.

'Alright, but the real test is if *I* sit on it.' I hauled myself onto the scaffold, and then squirmed onto the wall top – a seal with sunglasses flapping onto a wet rock.

'Uh oh. Here's the real test,' snickered Ahmet.

Celal scratched his head and chortled heartily at my expense. I'm afraid jokes and comments about weight aren't taboo in Turkey, which is exceedingly annoying at times. Sitting on the lintel, I gingerly slid my butt to the centre. 'Esra! Get a photo quick!'

Esra ran to the shed, grabbed my camera from its nail, and rushed back. She snapped twice before turning the gadget off. Relieved, I inched back to the wall, descended in as ungainly fashion as I'd climbed, and hit the ground with a thump.

'Looks like it works, folks. What a result!'

'Aye, woulda bin shit as a shitter's shitshed if it hadn't, eh?' Celal was staring at the lintel, a look of deep appreciation settling into his leathery features. Esra and I glanced at each other and then looked away quickly in case we sniggered.

We soon had the second lintel over the east window. Both were banged onto strip-anchors which were nailed into the earthbags below. The wall had climbed higher than my head (which admittedly, isn't very high). I was dismayed to see that the taller it became, the slower our progress. Whereas at the lower levels we'd reached an optimum speed of nearly three layers a day, at this level we were lucky to complete half that. At this rate, it would be Christmas before

169

I reached the roof. The first issue was hauling the bags up. With every metre, the bags became heavier to lift. On top of that, uncoiling those rolls of industrial barbed wire was vicious work. The barbed wire was usually my and Ahmet's job. He stuck a stick through the massive coil and walked backwards on the wall, while I weighted the wire down with rocks to prevent it from pinging up. I was always nervous I'd lose an eye, or become entangled in it and trip.

'So how are we going to fix the bags onto the lintels?' Esra was standing on the ground passing large stones up to me.

'We'll nail the wire onto the lintel tops.' I reached down for the next stone and promptly knelt on a barb. 'Ouch shit!' Sitting back up, I rubbed my knee. Esra winced in empathy, before continuing with her questioning.

'You mean it'll be like when we nailed the wire into the strip anchors at the door and window frames?' She was surveying the wall top thoughtfully.

'Exactly.'

'Oof ya! Come on, you two!' yelled Ahmet from a few yards ahead on the wall. 'This stuff is heavy!'

'Oh, just a minute, Ahmet!' Esra called up, and walked to the scaffold. 'Kerry, I have an idea. Let me do it.'

'Fine by me.' I stood up. I was glad to be as far away from the barbed wire as I could get. Esra clambered up to my spot, and I stepped past her to the scaffold and made my way back down. Once both my feet were safely on the ground, I looked up to see Esra with the hammer and nails in hand. I bent down to pick up a rock.

'No, I don't need the rocks. They're a complete waste of time. I'm going to nail it in place.'

And she did. It was the speediest, most elegant laying of barbed wire the world of earthbag has ever seen. She was so quick Ahmet couldn't unravel the coil fast enough. As I stood there agape, redundant rock in hand, she raised her hammer to me and grinned. 'OK, my turn for a photo, Kerry!'

I laughed, and made for the shed. 'Esra, I think you've just saved my butt.'

Esra took minutes to complete the ring. Ahmet stood at the back of the wall and nodded, impressed. Then he picked up the pliers and with a few grunts and groans cut the wire. I was standing below waiting for them to finish, when I heard a voice.

'Kerreeey!'

I turned round to see Dudu squatting on her observation rock, surveying the building site and grinning. She was wearing a pair of brown and green checked salwar pants, a pink crocheted cardigan and a blue polka-dot headscarf. I marvelled at the mishmash of fabric designs. 'Hello there neighbour!' I waved. It was then I noticed the silhouette of Adnan sauntering down the track behind her. Turning to the team I hissed. '*Mudur* is coming. Shit! Is everything lined up straight?'

'He he he,' chortled Dudu. 'So what's that chap Adnan going to find today, eh? There's always something. Always. He's got eyes like a hawk that one.'

I shook my fists at Dudu in pretend frustration and snickered. 'Let's take a tea break, folks,' I said beckoning the team.

As it happened, Adnan didn't find anything that day. He was preoccupied with something else: his earthbag building story. We were all sitting about the wooden table supping tea. Dudu was perched on a rock. I sat on a cushion next to her. Celal and Esra were hunched on stools, and Adnan sat astride the bench. Ahmet was off the land smoking.

'So, tell me. Why did everyone stop building mud and stone houses and start using concrete?' Adnan flicked the question over to Dudu. The creases on her little speckled face relaxed for a moment as she pondered. She pushed her lower lip out slightly, moved her false teeth about a bit and then spoke.

'Well, concrete came. And I spose we wanted to be modern, didn't we?' she said.

The Bulge

The first week of December came, and went, and the team reunited under a sun-gilded sky. By now, all the lintels were in place over the window and door frames, the stove pipe hole had been created, the windows were still wonky but I was at peace with that. We were on the last few bag layers before the roof, the prospect of which terrified me more than I care to say. I hoped this was the penultimate earthbag wall day.

'Yay! We're gonna make it,' cheered Adnan.

'Let's pull out all the stops and finish!' I was in team-rallying mode. Esra and I were back on our plank. Ahmet and Adnan were pushing up earth-filled bags for us to position.

'We're out of dirt an' all, so where am I gonna get it from now eh?' Celal was standing with the wheelbarrow and staring up at me, myriad wrinkles highlighted by the sunlight. I paused.

'Oof I don't know. Two more rows. Start digging a pool.'

'A pool?' Celal blinked.

'Yes, a pool. Right there next to where my tent is.'

Celal shrugged. Then he turned and trundled over to the tent platform. I saw him raise the pick and begin an onslaught on a grassy mound.

Our team carried on happily in this vein until the afternoon tea break. As we sat about the wooden table nursing our mugs, out of the corner of my right eye I spotted Adnan's fastidious gaze fixed on the front wall. He stood up silently. I turned away and stared at the view. The sun was hitting the needles of the thousands and thousands of pine trees, and they fluttered in the breeze like tall, green peacocks.

'Kerry, we have a problem.'

I groaned. I was starting to feel like the ground control supervisor of Apollo 13. Where did all these damn problems keep sprouting from? They were like wayward eyebrow hairs. Was there no end to them? I turned to Adnan. 'What now?' I snapped.

'I have no idea how we missed this. You guys were measuring with a plumb line when I was gone, right?'

'Of course!' I stood up indignantly. After the ubiquitous translation, Esra's eyes drew together outraged. '*Tabi ki!*' she said in Turkish, repeating exactly what I'd said.

'Well, I guess you weren't doing it, like top to bottom. Because if I let the plumb line drop from the top of *this* part of the wall...' And here Adnan climbed up on to our plank scaffold, then dropped the stone on the string that was our plumb line. 'You can see it's like...hell, Kerry! It's a good ten centimetres out! The front wall is *leaning*. Holy shit...this *can't* be good!'

I managed a good two minutes of stoicism before my self-control splintered. The definitive crack of my mood was probably heard as far as Dudu's house. I was simply too tired. Resting my head in my hands I pouted, suddenly feeling an irrational urge to locate a sledgehammer and start whacking slews out of the wall. As it happened, even if I had found a sledgehammer, the wall would have stayed standing. That's the way it is with earthbag roundhouses. I stood up and kicked the bag stand. After growling at the offending bulge for a minute or two, I plucked the tape measure from its nail in the shed. 'Alright, let's measure it!' I barked.

As humans are always more eager to learn of disaster than triumph, the team crowded round eagerly for a closer look. Esra was chewing her thumb while Adnan held the plumb line. I measured the distance from the base of the wall. It was near on 15 centimetres out. Sitting back on my heels I started to feel marginally persecuted. Obviously this was terrible. Walls are not made to lean. We needed a solution.

Earthbag building has prompted me to think a lot about problem-solving, because it's something one is engaged in on a regular basis when constructing a house. An issue arises, and it requires a solution, but there seem to be numerous paths to numerous solutions any one of which may or may not work. The road of problem-solving is both forked and deviant.

'I think we need to take all the bags off this section and rebuild,' said Adnan.

'I think you need to take a running jump,' I glared at the lean as if my wrath would somehow melt it into line.

'Kerry, you *can't* have a wall that leans out 15 centimetres. It's structurally unsound!' Adnan was losing patience.

'It will take us another two days to take the bags off and stick them on again. Be practical! I'm out of time, money and energy. There's *got* to be another way.'

'Well, if you'd spent a little longer measuring before you hurled all the bags up there, we wouldn't be in this mess.'

Ahem. This is an excellent example of the four century-old tussle between two classic philosophical approaches to problem-solving; rationalism and empiricism. Back in the days of the European enlightenment, rationalism was developed in its more modern form by philosophers like Descartes and Kant who sat for days in dark rooms, brows screwed up in pensive thought. Rationalism generally claims that knowledge can be independent of the senses. Problems can be solved like mathematical equations. Adnan was a good rationalist.

A little later in the 17th century, a mob of no-nonsense British philosophers developed an alternative – British empiricism. Empiricism has it that our knowledge of the world is derived primarily from the senses.

Crudely put, rationalists spend a lot of time in their heads, empiricists spend a lot of time experimenting, collecting physical evidence and making mistakes. Observe any problem-solving exercise and you'll see these two approaches, usually at loggerheads, coming to play. The rationalist has the theory, the empiricist wants to see it work in the 'real' world. The rationalist draws up plans and maps and ideas, the empiricist uses trial and error. Rationalists are tidy structured workers, empiricists make a mess and deplete resources.

Perhaps my British roots are to blame. Earthbag building made it clear to me, I tend to the empirical. This is why Adnan and I made a good team. Rationalism and empiricism work well together (in fact I'd say they can't in all feasibility work apart). The only trouble is, there are far too many occasions when neither of them solve the problem. The bulge was one such incident.

'Ah *birsey olmaz*.' It was Celal. He was scratching his head and squinting at the wall with what was left of his eyesight. *Birsey olmaz* was the mainstay of Celal's problem-solving technique, and it was liable to send me into an apoplectic fit whenever I heard it. It's a term local builders and workmen use on a daily basis, and translates literally as 'Nothing will happen' but basically means 'It'll be alright' when in fact there's a good chance it won't be alright at all. Your dog runs away to kill the neighbour's chickens, *birsey olmaz*. The roof of your bathroom dips in the middle, *birsey olmaz*. The taps are fitted back to front, a car hits your bumper, people fire rifles randomly over your head and yet apparently *birsey olmaz*. Once a tailor in Antalya snipped one leg of my trousers ten centimetres shorter than the other and said, '*birsey olmaz.*' So, you will understand that on apprehending these two Turkish words, I hear the theme tune to *Jaws* strike up.

'Celal, we've been through this. You can't just say *birsey olmaz* and hope for the best. We have a serious structural weakness here. What's going to happen when there's an earthquake?'

Celal shrugged, and nearly said *birsey olmaz* again, but refrained in the nick of time.

Ahmet, Esra and Celal were standing in front of the bulge, necks craned. Celal was scratching his head. Esra was biting her lip. But Ahmet's eyes were twinkling, and soon he began to chortle.

'Mud house, he he he. Told you. We should have used concrete. This wouldn't have happened then.'

'What's concrete got to do with it?' I glowered at him. He ignored me.

Anyway it'll be alright,' he said.

'Really? You think so?'

'Yeah of course. Stronger than an egg this house. Just give everyone crash helmets to wear when they come in. That'll sort it.'

There were muffled giggles all around. I shook my head and joined in the mirth. Well, what else could I do?

'I'll say one thing though,' Ahmet moved toward the rear of the house and patted the wall amiably. 'When you invite me round for dinner, I'm gonna be sitting nice and comfy at the back here, where the wall's straight.'

I think I might have said you should not start earthbag building without a cook. I'd like to add comedian to that super team of earth adventure. When everyone is beginning to lose it, it's the joker who saves the day.

'Oof. I'm going to talk to the trees,' I muttered, and stalked off toward the forest. I could sense the exchange of looks behind my back as I went.

It is at this juncture I'd like to introduce my favourite gizmo in the earthbag builder's problem-solving tool kit, one the 20th century thinkers often scorned, but earlier rationalists like Descartes gave a nod to. It always looks bad on paper, yet never fails to impress in practice: intuition.

No one gets far without intuition. There is an infinite cache of solutions surfing the width and breadth of the universe on frequencies that have no spatial or temporal correlation to where we are. Some might be deduced by inching step by step along a linear road of logical milestones. Some may be arrived at by a series of experiments. But the best solutions simply 'drop down' or spontaneously manifest. It's those clichéd light bulb moments.

Now, I said I was an empiricist. This isn't strictly true. Years of yoga teaching had infused the empirical foundations laid by my British education with a strong sense of mysticism (I apologise now to John Locke who is turning in his grave faster than a leg of lamb on a *döner* spit). Going to talk to the trees was my way of trying to access another, hitherto unseen slice of the knowledge pie. Celal nodded comprehendingly as I walked toward a great pine. Adnan's face became diplomatically expressionless. Ahmet grinned from ear to ear, because it meant he could smoke a cigarette. Esra stared at me intrigued.

Normally it worked. I'd sit quiet by a tree, or lay flat in the grass breathing in the magic dirt of nature around me, and something quite new would occur to me. I'd get a psychic nudge, or spot something I hadn't noticed before.

I'd hear a voice in my head or see an image. Then I'd know which step to take next. But this time, when I sat at the edge of the forest and waited for inspiration to descend, it was different. I closed my eyes, listened to the birds, smelt the damp earth. Nothing happened.

Time was passing. The branches on the trees didn't stir. The earth was silent. I looked about blankly. Fatigue had made my mind doughy. I was stuck in a museless pit without hunches or inspired flashes, and not so much as a solar powered LED flicker of light.

After ten minutes, I stood up defeated. Oh God. We really were going to have to take all the bags off, weren't we? Suddenly, I didn't have an ounce more fight in me. A bramble snagged in my hair as I picked my way through the bushes. I yanked it out along with a handful of hair strands and winced. Skidding rather ungainly into self-pitying melodrama, I muttered at the tree trunks, 'You've abandoned me!' They ignored me.

I walked out of the trees to find the team collected around the wooden table, heads gathered in discussion. It was about four pm and we only had another hour. The golden radiance that had crowned the morning had turned steely and cold, with a company of wolf shadows prowling over my land. I pulled a stool up to the table.

'Look, I need to sleep on this. Right now I'm not sure what to do. We've got an hour left. Let's make sure we've got plenty of earth ready, so that when we start again we can just motor on to the end.' I turned to Celal and Ahmet. 'You two dig as much as you can.'

They murmured their agreement and stood up.

'Esra, you tidy the place up. I know it's the Middle East but it doesn't have to look this bombed.'

'OK. I'll collect all the stray pots, bags and tools.' She raised both her fists in the air and stretched, then pushed her stool back and stood up.

'Adnan, let's check every part of the wall to see where we're leaning and where we're not.'

'Right.' Adnan nodded vigorously. Then he picked up the plumb line and clambered out of his seat. He climbed the wall, while I remained at ground level with the tape measure. We circled the building, checking each point. Though the front panel incorporated by far the most serious lean, most of the walls were out by 5–10 centimetres, with the exception of the back which by some miracle was dead straight. Ahmet had been right. That was definitely the space to shelter in an earthquake.

'So what are you gonna do then? Come on, Kerry, you can't have that front wall out by 15 centimetres. Jeez!' Adnan nimbly shinned down the wall to my level and handed me the stone on the string. I held it my grimy hand. Suddenly, I felt exhausted.

'Well, what I'm thinking is we could buttress it.'

'Man, that's gonna be ugly!'

'Oh don't say that! Maybe I can find a way to make it look nice?'

Adnan thought for a moment. We walked to the front of the building and studied the bulge. 'Hey, maybe you can make a buttress that, like curls.' Adnan traced a lovely spiral away from the wall. I watched him. Then I sat on the bench and laughed until my belly hurt. It was exactly the type of design I'd create, though God only knew if it would actually buttress anything.

Celal had pulled up a stool to the wooden table. 'So whatcha both planned then? I still say it'll be awright, if the bugger was gonna fall it woulda done it already. We've bin walkin' all over it for days. Snot even shaking. *Birşey olmaz!'*

I decided to change the subject.

'You know what? I'm taking a couple of days off and I'm going to head for the city for some inspiration.' Dusk was now upon us, drowning us in its ethereal fog.

'Sounds like a plan,' said Adnan. I'll get your story written up in the meantime.'

I turned to Celal. 'We're taking a couple of days off. I'm going to Antalya, and Adnan's writing our story up,' I translated.

Celal grinned, his moustache lifted to reveal a set of teeth that had seen far too much instant coffee and far too few toothbrushes. 'Wos the story called?' he said, pulling his woolly cap down over the tops of his ears.

I turned to Adnan and translated into English. He lowered his eyebrows and raised them again. 'I don't know. I don't usually choose the title, the editors do that.'

Swivelling back to my left, I ferried the conversation to Celal in Turkish. He sat for a moment fishing God knows what out of his teeth with his tongue. Then he laid his hands on the table, hands that were even grubbier than mine. He inhaled. 'Stubborn and Brave,' he said. 'That's what he should call it.'

Swinging back to the right, I conveyed Celal's title to Adnan. Adnan drank it in, nodding slowly. 'Yeah, that's...that's pretty good actually.'

**

The city was just what the doctor ordered. I spent two days with friends, dissecting the issue of the bulge from the comfort of a sunny restaurant. Oh the joy of meals arriving, and then the plates miraculously disappearing again. No wading through mud to turn the gas hob on, no washing up in freezing water, no chopping vegetables, no cooking.

The bulge proved an opportunity for each of my friends to unleash their creative powers. I was astounded by the wealth of ideas; there were bracing porches, earthbag flowerbeds that doubled as buttresses, earthbag seats, rock gardens, post and beam buttresses with grapevines climbing up them. I returned to The Mud rejuvenated and invigorated.

I walked onto my land in late afternoon the next day. It always felt different when no one else was around. Only in solitude could I truly sense its presence, hear it, connect with it. Dropping my rucksack on my tent platform, I inhaled the cool, pine-scented air. I noticed a robin perched on my composting toilet, red breast puffed up, little brown head jabbing this way and that. The tense vibration of the city left my bones and muscles as the hum of the natural world settled inside me.

Slowly, I circled the house coming to a standstill in front of the bulge. I now had a wealth of aesthetic design features exciting my imagination, but here in the physical reality of the thing, it looked different. I was out of money and time. Posts were expensive. Wood was expensive. Earthbags were cheap but time consuming and onerous. This is always the way. Ideas are the easy part. Realising them is where the mettle is required. I was, by this stage of the adventure, running low on fortitude.

The sky moved through the blue end of the light spectrum, from cobalt to indigo to violet. I sat in front of my house in the dirt and closed my eyes. The hardened earth was cool under my butt. It was always reassuring to recline on terra firma, and sense the mighty strength of the planet support one's tiny being. I tried to hear my land. What did she think? Was my house going to topple in the first earthquake? Or would it hold? Should I buttress the front? Or completely redo it?

At last I heard her. She guffawed like a coddling auntie from my toes right into my head. 'Why would I topple your house, my dear?' she said, 'when I invited you here to begin with?'

Just for the record, to this date, my house has survived three sizeable earthquakes. I'd say she danced through them. One these earth-shakers proved unexpectedly helpful. A few months after the house was completed, as the earth in my earthbag house settled, the right side of the lintel above the front door sank five centimetres. This left an annoying gap between one side of the door frame and the lintel. I was on the verge of finding some cladding to cover it when, as 'luck' would have it, the last quake pushed that part (and only that part) of my house up...by exactly five centimetres.

Make of that what you will.

***

The next day, Esra, Ahmet, Celal and I continued earthbagging as if nothing was happening. Esra and I had returned to our plank on the oil cans. The progress was tortuously slow at this height. Seeing that Ahmet was visibly struggling to lift sack after sack full of wet earth, Celal had joined him. Ahmet held the rim of the bag while Celal lifted from below. They plonked the fat orange beast onto our plank. Esra and I wobbled. We grabbed the shiny, wet polypropylene. On a one-two-three we both grunted and groaned as we pushed the bag onto the wall now two metres above ground.

'So what are we doing about the bulge then?' Esra asked while catching her breath.

'We'll just bring the final layers in a bit. Perhaps I'll buttress it later. Perhaps not. We'll see.'

The three Turks made no bones about it. A cursory glance about the Turkish countryside would explain why. Entirely straight buildings conforming to construction codes are so few and far between, they look out of place. This was of no comfort to Adnan though. He cantered past the compost heap straight after lunch, forehead puckered in disgruntlement. My throat clogged uncomfortably as I watched him steam toward the bulge. I felt as though I was about to be hauled up in front of the headmaster for cheating on a maths test.

From their respective positions about the wall, Esra looked on sympathetically and Ahmet's face was expressionless. Meanwhile, Celal avidly eyed the pair of us, anticipating conflict.

'So Kerry, what are you doing about that lean?'

I followed him to the front of the house, head bowed slightly. 'Erm, nothing right now.'

'Nothing?' The whites of his eyes expanded in outrage.

'I talked to the land. It's going to be fine.'

I must admit, if someone had said this to me, I would have probably reacted in much the same way Adnan did. He dropped his rucksack heavily by the wooden table and plonked himself onto a stool.

'Well I talked to Google and it's not gonna be in any way fine. It's a wonder the goddamn thing hasn't toppled already!'

I raised my shoulders by way of lame apology.

'I'm telling you, if a wall leans, it falls down. It's simple gravity! It's science. It's logic!'

I sat next to him and chewed my lip. For all intents and purposes it appeared he was right. I couldn't argue my case, because it wasn't founded on rationality. I stared at the bulge again. Termites of doubt sniffed the weakness in my resilience, and snuck inside. They burrowed into the supporting posts gnawing out tunnels of worry. What if he was right? Could I really rely on a few words I'd heard in my desperate, addled old head? I could feel my conviction buckling.

'Oh, perhaps I'll put buttresses up once we've got the roof on. I might make a rock garden just under the bulge to strengthen the lower part of the wall.'

Adnan shook his head in frustration. 'This isn't a plan, Kerry.' Then he turned away. 'Ah well, it's your house.'

It was just as I stared out over the valley, my eye following the red dirt track below as it snaked through the pines, I remembered a photo I'd seen of Chris' earthbag bungalows in Fethiye. It was a shot of one wall with a couple of plumb lines hanging down. I paused. Hurriedly, I stood up and walked to the shed. I grabbed my phone from the shelf and started to walk back to the table. Running through the names on the contacts, I located Chris and pressed the green button.

Ring. Ring. Ring. Ring.

I was still walking when he picked up. 'Hey there, Kerry, how's it going?'

'Like crap, Chris,' I said. 'And you?'

'All good here. What's up?'

So I explained about the wall and the lean. I asked if I should buttress it, or redo it, or tear the whole house down and give up. Chris listened. The phone crackled. Then he spoke.

'15 centimetres. Is that *all?*' I could make out a few chortles. 'Hey, our walls were out by at least 20 centimetres in places. Really tough to measure with the plumb line on a circular wall. But that's the awesome thing about round earthbag walls. They're indestructible. The entire structure is one interlocking wall, so it's impossible for a 'side' to fall out because there *are* no sides. The whole damn house would have to go.'

'Really?' I whispered. The sun was reappearing in my earthbag world.

'Know what? It's made me consider some freaky shapes, like I thought I might try a vase-like structure. Wouldn't that be cool?'

I agreed that would be very cool indeed.

When I put down the phone, I noticed Adnan scowling.

'Chris says his walls were 20 centimetres out and it doesn't matter,' I crowed, which was unfair of me.

'Hmph,' said Adnan. 'Chris isn't *God*, you know.'

Ooh. I swallowed a devilish little smirk. The Turkish part of the team had stopped all activity to hear the final verdict. I turned and explained the good news to them.

Celal stopped his digging. He clutched the spade handle in both hands as if he was pushing it like a pram. He nodded quietly. 'Told you,' he said looking vindicated. '*Birsey olmaz.*'

The Roof

The team broke up for a rest. For one thing we were exhausted. For another I was still trying to work out the details of the roof. And for yet another, I felt everyone was starting to become irritated with me, because I didn't know what I was doing, was desperate to finish, pushy and thus difficult. We really needed a stretch of a few days without anything going wrong. It was then that my dad, who must have telepathically obtained news of my predicament, offered me a trip home to England as a Christmas present. I took it. Just the thought of sleeping in a centrally heated room for two weeks, enjoying a piping hot shower *whenever I* wanted, slumping on a sofa and stuffing chocolate coated Hobnob biscuits in my mouth ad infinitum was therapeutic. I booked a flight for a little before Christmas. Adnan was flying to Afghanistan a few days ahead of me. He had another journo-mission to complete.

'I sure hope I see that mud plaster go on,' he was practising a contact ball routine. The glass sphere crawled up his arm, over his chest and onto the other arm like a transparent mouse. 'I need pictures.'

The temperature had once again dipped sharply, so I stayed in Adnan's spare room and spent the next week quietly panicking. The roof is arguably the most important part a building, and it usually costs nearly as much as the rest of the house. It is a shelter from rain and sun, and protects the building from the elements. On the Turkish

Mediterranean, if you have a decent roof, you can tack plastic up around the sides and feasibly survive. The trouble for me was, we'd moved away from earthbags (pioneer territory where no one knew any better than I did) to professional carpentry. I was treading water so far out of my depth, I couldn't even glimpse the sea bed.

If truth be known, I still hadn't decided what type of roof I was going to construct. This for a conventional builder is insanity, because the type of roof would necessarily dictate the rest of the building. I wasn't working top to bottom though. Like the natural world, I was growing bottom to top. Initially, I had set my heart on a beautiful reciprocal roof (reciprocal roofs are perfect for roundhouses as the beams extend upwards from equidistant points on the wall like a tepee). Adnan was motivated by the idea as well, and had embarked on a sketching and calculating bonanza. All of a sudden, rather than bug me, it comforted me. The two dimensional lines and angles were geometric safety rails on a precipitous learning curve that I couldn't quite decide whether I was climbing up or sliding down. I realised that unlike mud, carpentry is definitely a job for a careful rationalist. We worked out how long we thought beams should be. I drove to every logger's yard in the area. No one could supply me beams of the length required, within the time needed.

Back to square one.

'OK. I suppose I'll have to make a flat roof then. It's a gorgeous view up there. I can turn it into a platform to sit on,' I said knocking back a glass of wine. It was the same evening, and we were eating dinner. I was jumpy, but the wine was sanding down the harsher corners of my angst.

'How are you gonna do that?' Adnan peered up from behind his laptop and spooned some rice into his mouth.

I fiddled with my fork and began tapping my forehead with it like a reflex hammer. 'Oh, I don't know!' I groaned. 'I'm getting a bit overwhelmed by this.'

'Well let's have another look at Chris' bungalow roofs,' said Adnan. He moved the laptop mouse from left to right and clicked until he found it.

'I remember when I visited, they were going in rows, and I think he just banged plywood on top. But how far apart they were, I've no idea. And how did he make the roof round?'

'Hmm, here we are. Yeah it looks fairly straight forward. But how did the guy fix the rafters to the bags?'

'Ah, I read about that in the earthbag bible. It's strip anchors again, this time laid flat on the top layer of earthbags. The only thing I'm bothered about is something they keep calling a bond beam.'

'What's that?'

'Well, apparently it holds the entire structure together.'

Adnan's elbow was on the table top, his arm supporting the palm of his hand like a pedestal. He rested his head on it and screwed up his eyes. He was shaking with the kind of laughter people reserve for the aftermath of an earthquake, or when their house has gone up in flames. 'Right, so a bond beam is something vital then,' he expelled between shudders.

'Normally you put a ring of concrete round the top of the wall and this acts as a final lock-in for the bags. Obviously, I'm not doing it because it's concrete.'

'Obviously.' Adnan raised his head. 'What about making one out of wood?'

'But it's *round*. How could we do that? And more to the point, do we really need to?'

Adnan pushed the laptop away and leaned back against the wall. 'Well, I guess you'd better give your friend Chris another call then, eh?' He grinned mischievously. Touché my friend, touché.

I didn't only call Chris. I contacted anyone I could think of who knew something about building. People began to send in ideas for roofs. My uncle, a professional builder kindly mailed me a detailed roof plan with appropriate beam sizes. Chris told me he didn't use a bond beam, because it was so damn strong anyway it wouldn't fall apart.

But I couldn't sleep for worry. In the day I'd wander back to the house and stare at where the roof was supposed to be, lower lip dragging flaccid in awestruck horror. In the evenings I bothered Adnan relentlessly with all manner of questions: 'How much must it slope by? How will we make it slope? How can we carry the beams up there? How can I cut them to size? How will we attach them to each other?' In the nights, I spent hours lying in a rigid corpse posture, staring up into the darkness gripped by terror. I waded through dreams involving peculiar bending beams that wriggled out of their anchors, and an earthbag team that never turned up so that I'd have to keep finding them and driving them to the land, by which time one of the others would have disappeared.

Finally, the gallop of time squeezed me out of my paralysis. We were mid-way through December. I needed a roof. That was that. So it was one afternoon, I took a deep breath, emptied my bank account and purchased about 20 pine beams and 20 plywood boards. They arrived the next morning in the back of a truck that bumped and crashed down the fast deteriorating slope that was my road.

'Ah, you've been spendin' a whole wedge of money this week, eh?' said Celal as he hoisted the front of a beam onto his shoulder. His bobble hat gave him the air of a Smurf. I grimaced at him. I didn't even want to consider how much cash I had left and was entering the delusory zone of the financial ostrich. Lifting the back end of the beam onto my shoulder, I followed Celal down the slope to deposit the wood by the house. As I walked, dread crept through me like insidious puffs of mustard gas. Without warning, my faith left me. I felt incapable of leading the earthbag tribe. It was as though something had spent the last week puncturing me, and all my zeal and power had leaked out of the holes.

'Kerry, I'm going to coat this lot right away while you unload,' said Esra. She unzipped her jacket and eyed me knowingly. I nodded, grateful that someone else was making a decision on my behalf. Equipped with a huge can of wood protector and a roller, she pulled on some gloves and set about the beams with the kind of determination I was lacking.

By mid-morning we had unloaded the wood cargo. We stored the plywood boards inside the house and Esra started to paint them too. Now began the tortuous process of measuring where each beam would lay. I prayed Adnan would appear, grab a tape measure and take over everything, but it was far too early.

I climbed up to the top of the earthbag wall ready to start pulling up the rafters. Ahmet was on the ground pushing the beams up, while Celal and I sat on the top and yanked them across the structure. I remember sitting there, legs either side of the earthbags feeling sick with incompetence. I didn't know what I was doing. No one here knew what they were doing. This was nuts, completely foolhardy. I didn't even have enough money to effect an educational empirical mess up, because if we didn't manage a decent job with these rafters, or the idea didn't work, there was no more cash in the account to try something else. Would the rafters be secure on the bags? Should I have followed conventional wisdom and added a bond beam? I gulped as a vision of the roof sliding clean off the house and depositing itself on the mud like a vast plywood pancake, flitted through the front of my mind. I started taking shallow fitful breaths and blinking back tears of terror.

It was then while perched above the back door looking over at my olive tree, that I heard it loud and clear. My saviour! The words marched through my head like a battalion of misogynist hecklers. 'You'll *never* be able to do this.'

Well I'll be darned!

In that instant it was as though all the lights were switched on. It dawned on me why I was feeling so panicked and helpless. Never have I been so glad to hear those words. 'You'll *never* be able to do this' was a tiny linguistic box holding the entire gamut of my self-doubt. I could clearly see and hear 'You'll *never* be able to do this.' It was a conspicuous and unambiguous enemy. I remember holding a beam in my hands and thinking, 'Fuck! Now I have to be able to do this. I *have* to! Just imagine if I proved that arsehole right!'

Keeping your mind focussed in times of chaos is a valuable asset. 'You'll *never* be able to do this' was the bullseye on my mental dartboard. I girded my loins, buckled up and quarried some confidence back. 'Roof, you are going on whether you like it or not,' I growled to no one in particular. 'I'll give you, *you'll never be able to do this*. And it will be long and sharp and you can stick it right up your macho arse.' I repeated this every time I dropped a beam in place.

I'm sure the feeling that you're not up to the job afflicts everyone who builds, male or female, professional or amateur. We've all of us been disempowered by a system that likes to hold us hostage with horror stories and doubt. Something goes awry and suddenly our worst fears appear to have been confirmed. We become paralyzed by a lack of self-belief.

Now, I said the roof was the most important part of a building, didn't I? I erred. Willpower is the most important part of your building. Determination is your roof. Your rafters are made of gumption. If you possess these, you will survive any storm that comes your way. If you don't? Give up now and save yourself a lot of time and money. My advice to anyone who suffers an attack of the knee-knockers while building is to think of some smarmy know-it-all who told you, you couldn't do it. Just picture them mocking you, feel inordinately aggrieved, face them off and shoot them down in your mind's eye. It's incredibly therapeutic, and if nothing else it will at least give you something other than failure to think about. As an acupuncturist in Taiwan said to me, 'Anger is a very powerful and useful energy, if you can only channel it to create rather than to destroy.'

The Rafters

'I love it up here, don't you?' I said to Esra the next day.

The view from the roof was exquisite. A white tide of mist ebbed in the dark folds of the valley below, the vapour streaked silver by the sunlight above. In contrast, the pine slopes had turned from emerald to the colour of kale. The sun was so bright the sky was shimmering. Below us, we could see Celal and Ahmet heaping barrow-loads of dirt onto a sheet of plastic, preparing for the earthplaster.

'Oh yes. You definitely want a platform up here. You can drink tea and read books to your heart's content. All quiet, no one to bother you.' Esra pulled out the hammer like a club and bashed a hefty nail into the flat square of wood that was acting as a strip anchor.

One of the most rewarding aspects of building with your friends is that when it's all over, your house becomes a testament to the people who built it. Each part of your home holds a fond memory like a locket on a chain, or a photograph in a wallet. When I look at my floor, I see Ahmet sawing non-stop for a day and a half. When I regard my stone walls it's Celal's hands I see, when I consider the foundations I remember Annika shovelling the gravel into the bags, when I gaze at the walls I remember Esra and me standing on our plank knocking earthbags in place. And the roof? Well, despite my fretting, it turned into a thing of great beauty and strength. I look at the precision with which the rafters were laid and the neat application of the brackets (all are dead in line, not a millimetre out), and I smile and remember Adnan.

'Oh my God! How does Adnan do that?' Esra had a garden-gloved hand over her mouth. I looked up from my perch on top of the wall. Adnan was half-way across a rafter. He sauntered over it like a professional tight-rope walker. Adnan's involvement in circus wasn't only limited to contact ball, apparently.

'Just warning you, Adnan, if you fall and break your leg you can't sue me. I'm happy to say the scourge of litigation hasn't reached Turkey yet,' I quipped.

'As if I'm gonna fall now, Kerry, come *on!*'

He reached our side of the wall. We had now created a type of grid structure with the beams. I had two 20-by-10 centimetre whoppers running east to west. The rest of the 5-by-15s were laid north to south over these two. Esra and I were at either ends of these rafters attaching them to the strip anchors. I used the drill to fix each beam to each strip anchor. Adnan measured where they should sit and Esra whacked nine inch nails into the anchors driving them into the earthbags below. We were on the last one.

'We're gonna start fixing each rafter to the support beams now, right?'

'Yes, Adnan,' I groaned. 'Aw it looks such a tedious job! I just don't have the patience for this carpentry stuff.'

Adnan was now sitting beside me. Esra had moved to the other side of the wall to hammer in the last anchor.

'Kerry, I have an idea.'

'Oh yes?' I drove in the last screw. The drill stopped its whining. I loved my drill. In fact I love all power tools. I love that they've made muscle power obsolete and me independent. Manufacturers of power tools really haven't cottoned on how to market DIY tools to women. They have assumed women are not interested in buying them. They make them all look like weapons or phallic symbols (or both), stick them in Neanderthal workman type boxes and generally fail to create sleek, lightweight, easy to use products. This is both their loss and mine. My humble lithium-powered, cable-free Mac Allister drill remains my favourite hand tool of all time, not least because the suppliers added a superbly efficient LED torch powered by the same batteries and packed it in an easy to carry blue fabric case that doesn't bash your knees every time you take it out. But the best of it is, those batteries (two of them) take 20 minutes to charge, and last hours. When you're off the grid or using solar power, durable batteries is what you need.

I lifted up the drill and exhaled a contented sigh of fulfilment. 'Fire away, what's your idea?'

'Well, Esra is so goddamn capable. I don't think she's ever used a drill. I'm happy to show her how while we attach the rafters to the support beams.'

I grinned and handed him the drill. Atta boy!

It was a heart-warming sight; Esra perched on the rafters drill in hand, driving those babies home with Ahmet looking on from below, slightly envious. I thought he might have shuffled his feet a bit. But I'll say this for him, in a land where women are rarely allowed to outshine their husbands, he let her have her moment. In future years, when the pair of them had a baby boy and established a greenhouse of tomatoes, it was in fact Esra who ran the greenhouse while Ahmet took care of their son. He climbed about 50 notches in my estimations as a result.

Rounding the Square

'Oof, how the hell am I going to create a decent circle up on that roof? I've got to cut the beams to size too.' I was sitting in Adnan's house, which by now had become my second home, engaged in the unbelievable. I was clutching a pencil and paper, and sketching how to round a square. I had never thought it would come to this: a house plan.

Adnan squinted over my shoulder. 'You outlined the circle for the house using a stick in the ground and some line, right?'

'Yup, but on the roof I don't have anywhere to attach the string to. Unless...I know, I'll stick a few plywood boards up there temporarily to create a bit of a platform, and bang a nail in the central point. Got it!'

'How you gonna cut the beams down to size?'

'There's only one thing for it,' I said throwing the pencil down and folding my arms. 'The chainsaw.'

Adnan eyed me dubiously. '*Jeez*! I don't like that thing down at ground level. So you're gonna balance precariously on a rafter on the top of your house, start up the motor and chainsaw the beam in a perfect straight line? Holy shit!'

'Do you have a better idea?'

'No. Just don't lose a leg, eh?'

When you build a round house, rounding the square is something you seemed to be involved in on a regular basis.

It can become rather tiresome. Every item of building material on the market today is designed for squares or rectangles or straight lines. Nothing is designed to curve, bend or be round. So with this in mind, why bother with a house that's round at all?

I've already mentioned the strength factor of the circle. With a straight line or a straight wall, the centre-most point is weaker than the ends. After our winter deluges on the Turkish Mediterranean, I often came across broken stone walls. This is because nowadays they are making two significant errors in wall construction: 1. They use concrete without adequate drainage, which means the water banks up behind the wall creating a huge amount of pressure. 2. They build straight walls. Back in the old days, terracing walls were cobbled out of dry stone, and they arced in pretty semicircles. There was a very good reason. Arcing walls distribute the pressure, just as circles do.

This is all well and good, but my lust for a circle wasn't ultimately founded on a desire for strength. It was about aesthetics. Many architectural schools advocate the psychological benefit of avoiding straight lines; from Hundertwasser to feng shui, paths, walls and interior design are supposed to flow. When this happens the eye is guided smoothly from zone to zone without the abrupt switches in visual stimuli created by corners and squares. This may all seem a little abstract for someone who just wants a shelter, but today as I sit in this mud circle and type my story, I can attest that the roundness inspires me. If my gaze is drawn to a spot on my earth wall, it moves smoothly to the next detail and then is carried on to the next in a never-ending circular movement. If you've never experienced sitting in a roundhouse, this won't make much sense. But personally, there is nowhere I'm more creative than within this wall.

Circles are also soothing, which inevitably attracts manic, driven types like myself. The round, nubbly walls create a cave or womb effect. A nurturing-type energy is generated within a circle, as opposed to the more structured atmosphere of a square or rectangle. In a world which is by and large underpinned by masculine values, it's refreshing to live in a space ordered by the feminine, where curves predominate over erections, and soft lines precede hard angles.

This is all fine and dandy of course, until you try building.

***

The next morning, it was only Celal and me on the land. The rest of the earthbag team had other things to do. The sun – oh we had so much sun that December – slipped in and out of the few puffs of cumulus scudding through the blue. The vista pulsed from dark olive to chartreuse as though it were blushing.

'Right, you climb up onto those plywood boards, Celal, because you're the lightest.' I was looking up at Celal on the top of the wall from inside the house through the grid of the rafters. My hands were cupped over my eyes to shade them from the sun's intermittent glare.

'Righto,' Celal said and shinned across the beam to the island of plywood we'd laid in the centre of the roof. Apo the dog wandered into the house. He shook his coat sending clouds of beige fur everywhere. Then he sat directly under my feet.

'OK. Now, we'll measure east to west, and then north to south and find the centre,' I declared confidently.

'Giss the tape measure then.'

I threw it up and proceeded to watch Celal squat on his haunches in the centre of the roof with the tape measure, lob the end at the east wall, throw it again because it didn't quite reach, be quite content with the fact that the tape measure was twisted and pitched at an angle, drag the measure along a beam in the direction of the east wall, watch the end ping from its position, hold the measure mid-air at that point and declare, 'It's about four metres till 'ere.' Then continue measuring from that imaginary mid-air coordinate to the west wall, add, 'And it's about three metres till 'ere,' and sit down waiting for further instructions.

I sighed. Then I climbed over Apo and made my way to the scaffold we'd made. I shinned up to the roof muttering quietly to myself, 'If yer wanna job done properly...'

Apo followed me with his dopey gaze and shook his big Anatolian head. I got the impression he thought this was all a bad idea.

An hour, a ball of string and a barrel full of swearing later, we had found our centre. Celal proudly drove a nail into it as though he was sticking a flag into a summit. We punched the air and cheered. We both watched Apo sidle out of the house through the front door. He gawked up at us and shook his head again.

'Ha ha ha, he's wundring what the devil them humans are doing, I reckon.'

'*I'm* wondering what the devil we're doing a lot of the time, Celal,' I chortled. We sat back for a minute and admired the view. I could clearly see the curl of the seafront over in Alakir 25 kilometres away, with its spatter of miniscule box-buildings overpowered by the two mountains at either edge of the bay. I turned back to Celal. 'OK, next job is to get some more string and a pencil and find the circle. You hold the string in place with the nail and make sure it doesn't pop out of position, I'll go round the wall and mark each beam.'

'Right you are.' Celal saluted.

214

Another hour, plenty of bruises and some close encounters with broken legs later, I had marked where the circle edge was on each beam. Now all I had to do was lop off the ends of the rafters with the chainsaw. It sounded so straightforward. But Celal and I were drooping at the edges slightly and it was something that could only be remedied by tea and biscuits.

The kettle was soon hissing on the stove. I waded into the 'kitchen' and poured the hot water into a flask. Then I dumped it onto the table. Celal pumped the water onto the sugar coated teabag nestling at the bottom of his mug and exhaled a happy workman's sigh.

'Ah, that's better innit? So how you gonna cut them beams, then?'

'With the chainsaw,' I said. Celal looked up at the roof, then back at me, and said nothing.

We were sitting with the sun on our faces sipping from our mugs, when Adnan's voice wafted down from the road. 'Hey! How's it going?'

I turned round. 'Where the hell were you when the finicky perfectionist measuring crap needed doing?' I raised my mug to him.

Adnan lit a cigarette and surveyed our efforts at rounding the square from his usual vantage point on the road behind the house.

215

'Looks good from here. It's actually pretty genius how you've rounded it,' he said.

I puffed up in self-satisfaction. Adnan screwed the end of his cigarette up and slipped it in his pocket. Then he wandered down to the site. 'So it's chainsaw time now, eh?' he called over.

I postponed the dreaded chainsaw moment for as long as was feasibly possible. But finally the time came. Leaving the tea table, I scuttled over to the shed. Dragging the machine out, I filled it with petrol and oil. Then, I handed it to Celal. Once I'd clambered up onto the top of the wall, I found my first rafter. It was a smooth pinewood beam jutting from the front of the house, and I had to sit astride it and grip it between my thighs. Celal stood on the oil drum scaffolding and passed up the machine.

I moved back to the thick earth walls to start the chainsaw up. She whirred and growled like an enormous mechanised and deadly mosquito. As I stood up, wobbling slightly, a flood of appalling images cascaded into my mind; there was one of the chainsaw flying out of my hand and slashing someone on the ground to bloody pieces, one of me falling headlong off the house with the chainsaw still whirring – it was a toss-up as to whether I fell onto the blade or not, there was one of me slipping and the chainsaw jolting back up to carve my head in two, and another image of me sawing straight through my foot. The trouble with chainsaws is there's so much that can go wrong.

I took a deep breath and edged along the beam. My heart was thumping like a man buried alive hammering on his coffin door. The tension was palpable. My hair stood on end, my teeth were on edge and my toes were screwed up in anticipation. I began to sweat. The boys on the ground were silent. Everyone was focussed on that whirring chain of destruction.

Perching on one beam, I could just about reach its neighbour with the saw. I made myself as stable as is possible when you're balanced on a rafter, released the safety catch and let the blade fly. Minutes later the beam had been shorn down to size. I cut the engine.

'It ain't straight though,' pointed out Celal.

'No, that won't do at all, Kerry,' chimed in Adnan. 'Look, it's a real mess.'

Shaking a little I moved off the rafter and back to the security of the wall. That was before I deposited a deluge of bad language upon the pair of them in. It was the verbal equivalent of upending a slop bucket.

'What the fuck! You bastards think you can do better then get your arses up here and do it!'

I jumped down from the wall. Apo was under my feet for the umpteenth time that day. So I shouted at him too. He gave me such a wounded look, I calmed down.

'I don't like it when you chainsaw,' ventured Adnan five minutes later, still picking the figurative potato peelings and eggshells out of his hair. 'It makes you a bit aggressive.'

I slumped onto one of the stools about the table and slugged a glass of water. Then I sulked for a minute or two. A buzzard swooped overhead, its mottled wings splayed in a wide, feathered arc. It looped round and round, searching for a mouse or a wayward chicken. By the looks of things it was having a bad day. Rising and falling, the bird swirled like a broken kite, out of my line of vision.

I hunched up. I was ashamed at my outburst. 'Aw, I'm sorry, guys,' I said. 'It's just so stressful. And no one else is willing to get up there and do it, are they?'

Adnan shook his head. Celal never touched the chainsaw anyway and said he didn't know how to use it. I looked up at the rafter. It was indeed a mess. The edges were frayed and it wasn't cut straight. It looked as though a giant, joist-skipping beaver had gnawed through it. Turning from the rafter, my eye moved to my hammock. The afternoon light had caught the edge of one of the less illustrious olives that it was tied to. It brought out the best in the sinewy, old tree. I noticed attractive knots and arcs where before I had only seen dying wood and flaking bark. The leaves were dusted with sunlight and twinkled pluckily.

Standing up, I made my way over to where Celal and Adnan were loitering. 'Now what?' I grumbled. The three of us were standing under the jagged beam, necks craned. Celal coughed.

'Aye, I think I can saw 'em off by hand,' he said. He stuck both hands on the waistband of his jeans which were not quite held up by the piece of string he'd used as a belt, and hitched them up.

'*Really?*' I turned to him gracing him with a look of such awestruck gratitude he might have been The Second Coming.

'Yeah. If you can hold one end of the saw, we can do it together. We'll get them buggers straight.'

And that's what we did. The three of us clambered up to the roof. Sometimes Adnan took the other end of the saw, sometimes I did. It took all day, but we managed it. By evening, once Celal had left, Adnan and I sat our bums on the pine needle covered ledge behind the house. All the beams had been cut to create a wonderful circular grid. It looked fantastic, if I say so myself.

'Hey, really sorry I shouted at you, brother. It wasn't OK. I apologise,' I offered meekly and rested my back against the trunk of a pine.

'Ah, it's alright, Kerry. Adventures like this can get intense. That's what it's all about, right?' He smiled and passed me a roll-up. 'So what's tomorrow's job then?'

'First, we're going to unroll the bamboo matting over the beams, and then nail the plywood on top. Don't ask me how we're going to do it, Adnan. I haven't a damn clue.'

'Well, knowing you, and knowing this project, it'll somehow all work out.'

I nodded. Knowing me and knowing my land, it would.

***

The next morning Celal trotted merrily on to the land with Apo bringing up the rear. He wore a woollen tank top over his shirt, and a knitted hat pulled over his ears. But there was something wrong. His face was a mesh of panic lines.

'Sgonna rain!' he called out frantically as he picked his way past the tower of lime packets that lined the entrance. Apo sniffed and cocked his leg over the bags, just in case any other dog in the vicinity should claim them as their territory.

'Are you serious?' I stared at the sky. The blobs of white cloud floating aimlessly over the cobalt above looked utterly benign.

'That's what the telly said. It's coming in after midday. And it's gonna be a howlin' piss bucket when it does.'

'A howling piss bucket...Oh dear, that doesn't sound good.'

'So let's get going! We need to hammer those plywood buggers down as fast as we can.' Celal was already shinning up the scaffold to the roof as he spoke.

'But I don't really know how we're going to do this. We need to think!' I cried up.

'No time for thinking! Throw up the hammer.'

I didn't like the direction this was taking. More haste, less speed and all of that. 'But the bamboo is going *underneath* the plywood,' I shouted up. I'd seen this method of creating a ceiling from Chris, but had no idea how he'd actually put the thing together. The aim was to lay the bamboo on the rafters, and then nail the boards over the top.

Celal's head appeared over the wall. 'You mean them rolls over there? Ah, wondered what they were for. OK push 'em up then.'

Shaking my head, I walked over to the large rolls of bamboo matting, threw one over my shoulder and staggered with it to the back of the house where Celal was leaning over. I tipped the roll up against the wall, knelt and pushed from the bottom, Celal grabbed the top and it landed with a smack on the rafters. He dragged it to the front of the house and gave it a little push. It unravelled like a massive, husked toilet roll and smoothly covered a 2-by-5 metre strip of what was about to become my roof. I walked into the house via the back door and stared up. It looked divine. Sometimes things run so smoothly you can't believe your good fortune. I clenched my fists and waved them in the air cheering.

'OK, now drag a plywood board over the top of the matting. Let's see if it works.'

Celal promptly grabbed one of the large rectangles and dragged it over the bamboo. It sat neatly in place. Not only that, but due to some fluke of proportions that stagger me, the plywood boards happened to fit exactly to the width of three rafters. (No, I hadn't measured this previously, and yes, I know I should have done.)

'Celal, I think you should know. We are perched at the starting edge of a lucky day. Let's milk it!'

'Hammer and nails!' said Celal fully focussed. I threw them up.

By lunchtime, the centre of the roof was all but complete. We had unrolled the bamboo and banged down the majority of the boards over the top. All that was left was the edges. It was going to be another exercise in rounding the square. Each board would have to be held in place. I'd have to drag the string and pencil round and draw a curved line on it, then we'd have to remove the board, saw it by hand, then replace it and nail it down.

Celal trotted off home for lunch. Meanwhile, I sat on the front step of my house. It felt wonderful to squat there; the first true action of home dwelling I'd committed. Munching a corner of bread, I surveyed my 'queendom'. Ah, life was good! It was very good indeed. I pretended not to notice that the sun had now disappeared behind a wedge of thick grey stratus. A wind had picked up as well. The pine trees were rustling in agitation. The birds were flitting about as if time was of the essence. But I almost had a house, so I didn't care.

Once I'd eaten I climbed up onto the roof again. I found our 'centre' nail and tied a new length of string to it. Then I taped the pencil to the string.

'Ahoy!' It was Celal. He hopped over Dudu's fence rather than walk all the way round. His lunch break was over.

'Perfect timing! I need you to hold this board.'

Celal zipped up to the roof. He grabbed a square of plywood and held it in place while I stretched the string and drew part of the large circle on it. Once it was marked, we yanked the board to the centre of the roof that was already hammered down. Celal positioned the saw. I steadied the other end. We slid through the plywood quickly, and I was surprised by the smoothness of the cut. It was looking good. Excitedly, I carried the curved board over to its slot on the roof-jigsaw. Celal and I nailed it in place. We both nodded.

Mission accomplished. Only ten or more so to go. I shivered slightly as a cool gust rushed over the roof. Celal pulled his hat down a little. Looking north to the back of the house, I gulped. The sky was a swamp.

'Aye, it's comin' in,' said Celal.

'Yup, you were right. We're going to have to go at it hammer and tongs now. Oh God!' I squeaked.

Celal reached behind him. 'Here's the next board.'

We worked with the kind of fury you only experience when your life depends on it. We took no breaks and marched about the roof like a pair of lithium-charged super-roofers. Four boards were down. Then five. Then six. A clear circle was manifesting and it looked so incredibly sweet I wanted to hug it. But the darkness in the north was galloping towards us, the sky at the back end of the house swollen with oncoming calamity. Celal and I had long ceased to chat. I was filled with excitement and trepidation in equal measure. As the seventh board hit the deck, I wondered if we'd make it, because if we didn't, my house was going to become Yapraklı's answer to Aquaworld.

'Oh my God, it looks *awesome!*' the voice fluttered down from above as though gliding on the wings of celestial beings. I looked up at the mud track and at the dark figure peering at us from it. Then I leapt up and cheered.

'Adnan! You are *bang* on time.' Talk about saved by the devil.

'Yeah, look at that weather coming in.'

'We've got three more boards to go.'

'I'm on my way up.'

I clapped my hand to my forehead and fell back on the roof expelling an infantile gurgling sound. Celal grinned and shook his saw in the air. '*Mudur Mudur*!' he yelled.

So, while Adnan and Celal sliced through the boards, I measured and drew the part-circle on the next one. This speeded the process up considerably. Two boards were fixed. As soon as I'd finished measuring the last board, I sent Celal down to haul up the tarp while Adnan and I cut the last board into shape. I have a clear image of the pair of us sawing like crazy with storm clouds the colour and size of demonic spirits hovering above us. As we banged down that final board, and Celal carried up the tarp, the first spatters of rain hit the deck. By now we were galloping. Celal and Adnan opened the plastic sheeting while I cleared the roof of tools and nails and other debris. Fighting a pugnacious wind, we managed to spread the plastic and nail it cursorily in place. We jumped down from the roof and hid in the house. It was then that the heavens opened and The God of Mud said, 'Time's up!'

The three of us stood in the house. A plastic sheet still covered that enduring juniper floor. There was no glass in the windows, and they were wonky. The walls rippled with plump orange sacks rendering my home bunker-like. Even so, the emotions that welled inside me as I stood, for the first time, and experienced my earthbag house as a shelter, were exquisite. I poked my head out of the back door frame and watched the water pouring from the back of the house. Celal and Adnan were inside, heads tipped back, scouring the roof for leaks. So far, there weren't any.

'So when yer movin' in then?' Celal grinned at me.

'Well, not yet. We've got to get the plaster on first. And the floor. I keep falling into the pits at the edges.'

'You'll finish laying those floorboards after the plastering, I presume,' said Adnan bending over to study the large dips in the tarp where we'd left the boards free. I nodded. I swore that damn floor would be the very last thing I hammered.

'Esra and Ahmet are free again next week so we can get 'em to help with this plaster. Should 'ave it done in a jiffy.'

'Yeah!' I said. 'We'll throw it up before I fly out to the UK for Christmas, and by the time I get back it'll be dry. Then all I have to do is tack up some plastic on the doors and windows for now, and move in! Brilliant!'

The men nodded approvingly as we made our way to the door and out into the rain. Oh optimism. And oh those famous last words...

The Lath Coat

Earthplastering is an art. Just like stonemasons and carpenters, there used to be a wealth of earthplasterers – artisans who knew the earth of their locality like the back of their skilled, dirt-stained hands and had perfected the art of rendering a mud finish out of it. Alas, they are no longer, which can leave us newbie natural builders wading in circles around a signpostless bog. Plaster composition changes considerably depending on your climate, the clay content of your dirt and the type of clay. It's not something you can simply look up in a book or research online, because it's region specific. Once you *have* discovered the correct mixture, earthplaster is added slowly and gradually to your building. Like knowledge or learning a new skill, it is accumulated layer by layer, each one anchored by the one before. Woe betide you if you rush it.

We only took one day's rest. Time was of the essence. Adnan, who had already reached far beyond the call of volunteer duty, now needed to complete the story. He stayed at home shackled to his computer, a little regretfully if I may say so. Building an earthbag house may be exhausting, but there's no doubt about it, it's joshing good fun.

The rain didn't last long, and it left a gift in its wake. Now that the earth was wet, we needed less water. This meant my infernal drives up and down the jarring, rock-strewn declivity of my road became mercifully less frequent. That morning, our pile of pre-prepared earth plaster sat on a large rectangle of tarp. Ahmet and Celal had pulled back the plastic covering and were staring at it in appalled wonder. It looked as though a herd of prehistoric mammoths had mysteriously wandered onto my land and defecated en masse, leaving them to work out what to do with the manure. The cack slobbered and blubbered under their gaze like the mud embodiment of Jabba the Hutt.

'I think we should give it another mix before we start throwing,' I said. Ahmet groaned. He mooched over to the shed and pulled out a pair of wellington boots. I had my own pair already on. Celal stood at the edge of the tarp with a spade. I waded into the centre of the small mud mountain and began to stomp. Ahmet followed suit.

Churning mud plaster may look a bit of a lark, and in many respects it is. There's plenty of slop, and cavorting with a pile of mud can be a mirthful fraternising experience. But it's also hard work. If you want thighs that will crack a walnut, I highly recommend it. Ahmet, for one, didn't aspire to walnut-cracking thighs.

'Pff. We need a cement mixer, that's what. This is knackering.' He was red in the face and perspiring. I couldn't even reply, I was that tired. Celal moved around the edge of the tarp and shovelled the dung back into the centre while we mud gophers paddled slower and slower. Eventually, I staggered out of the ring, Ahmet close on my heel. I collapsed on the ground feeling my legs tingling with fatigue.

'That'll have to do. When's Esra coming back?' I wailed.

'She'll be 'ere tomorrow don't you worry about that. Let's load up your wheelbarrow and start lobbing this crap onto the house.' Celal wandered off to fetch the barrow while Ahmet and I recovered. I heard him jangling and bumping round the earthbag circle. 'So we gonna add lime to it, or what? I say it needs lime,' he called as he approached. There was a certain conviction in his voice.

'The earthbag bible doesn't mention anything about adding lime at this stage. The lime is for the final coat.'

Celal pulled his eyebrows a bit lower and drew his lips tightly together. He'd had enough of the earthbag bible with its new-fangled techniques and its weird foreign ways. 'Let's make a few test patches, some with lime, some without, and leave 'em a few days and see what happens.'

This was of course what we should have done weeks ago. Never, ever, *ever* cover your entire house in a mud plaster you haven't tested. It's akin to cooking a banquet without any clue of the ingredients. The trouble was, I had become complacent. As far as I was concerned, the hardest part of the construction was over. I had succeeded in engineering a house and was quite sure this mud plaster malarkey was going to be as easy as whipping up a chocolate pudding.

'Alright, Celal,' I sighed from my prostrate position under the olive tree. 'You make up some batches and slap them on the far wall. We'll check them later and see how they turn out.'

Celal scurried off and found a yoghurt pot, mixed some lime and produced some experimental concoctions, while Ahmet and I found our legs again.

A few minutes later Celal was done, and we were ready for what is known in the trade as the lath coat. This is the primary layer of earth plaster used to fill in the gaps between the bags. You throw large mud patties into every niche you can find, and then squash it in with your fingers leaving the plaster rough and nobbled so that your next layer can attach to something. Celal shovelled plaster from the limeless dung pile into the barrow. Ahmet and I scooped it up and began hurling mud balls at the walls. We both agreed this was far more exhilarating than stomping in it.

'There are a lot of stones in here,' I commented as I rummaged in the barrow of muck.

'Aye. They were in the clay. Couldn't get 'em out. But it didn't matter in the earthbags, did it?' Celal stuck his hand in the barrow and gave it a cursory stir.

'Do you think there's enough straw? I can't see hardly any.'

'Can put some more in if yer like.'

I shrugged. 'OK. Throw a bit more in.'

As must be excruciatingly clear, we were eons from any sort of precise measuring. Adnan would have gnashed his *mudur's* teeth had he seen. A yoghurt pot more straw was added to the barrow and stirred. Ahmet and I continued the sport of mud ball and were soon covered in brown spatters. The sun plunged down the black spine of the mountains with a haste that was alarming. The shortest day of the year was looming. Before we'd cleared up, the site was consumed by the murk of evening, but a good three quarters of the gaps were filled, so I was happy. Things were progressing just as they should, so I thought.

The next morning, the sun was heckled by a few hardy wafts of mist. But by nine o'clock they had evaporated leaving the sky beaming and the trees dancing in green, sequinned bodysuits. The entire earthbag team, bar Adnan, had assembled and we were attacking that plaster with zeal. Celal shovelled batches into the two barrows, while Esra, Ahmet and I stood at various points around the house playing our merry mud ball game. Volleys of patties were hurled at the orange sacks accompanied by a satisfying squelch with each direct hit. By the first coffee break our lath coat was complete, and Jabba the Hutt looked as though he'd had his stomach stapled. Gone was the mountain of mud blubber. All that was left was a small hillock. Esra peered at it dubiously. 'We need more plaster, now!' she bellowed over at us before folding the plastic cover back over it.

Celal counted five sugar cubes into his tea and clanked the teaspoon around the mug. He looked over at the humble plastic-covered dune. 'Aye, that'll be this afternoon's job. Thing is, when I watched that bloke over by the English, he left the plaster a week or more and kept churning it over and over again.'

'You've watched someone do this before?' I put my mug down and fixed my gaze on Celal. The man was a trove of secret information. Why hadn't he mentioned this earlier? I pondered briefly whether my obsession with the earthbag bible and the internet had stultified his faith in local knowledge and the hands-on methodology of regional artisans.

'Yeah, the English put earth plaster on their walls.'

'But the walls are concrete,' I squinted at him confused.

'Aye, but they wanted a natural look inside so this bloke came from over yonder, paid him a fair whack I can tell yer, and he did it for 'em. Some of it fell off though.'

'Because concrete holds the damp.'

'Aye.'

'Well, we don't have time to stomp the mud for weeks, Celal. We'll just have to take a chance.'

Celal took a final swig of tea and banged the cup on the table. 'Yeah, it took that fella ages. Forget it, *birşey olmaz.*'

I brushed off the many implications of what Celal was saying, because I had set my heart on moving into my house by the time I returned from my Christmas trip to the UK. I let nothing tamper with that vision. Having just clawed a house from the earth using willpower and force of mind, I now believed resolve was the answer to everything, the bulldozer for every hump to arise on the building road. I could feel my guts tightening into a hard ball. It wasn't a mud ball. It was an iron pellet. There is a fine line between determination and foolish obstinacy, and I was becoming sloppy in my distinctions.

After the break, Ahmet and Celal began a frantic dirt collecting mission. Without waiting for the first layer to dry, Esra and I used the remainder of the plaster to begin a second coat. The plaster was about ten centimetres thick in places. After we had covered the front panel, Esra stood on a ledge and smoothed the plaster with a wet sponge.

'Ooh it's like icing a giant cake, isn't it?' she said smiling as she massaged the muddy wall. I found a new pair of rubber gloves and pulled them on with a thwack. Then I joined her. It was therapeutic to let my hands glide over the muddy wall, almost as though the house was alive and enjoying our touch. As the day closed its shutters, I stood back and admired our handiwork. The front panel looked a dream. The earthbags had disappeared and the worst of the lumps were hidden. It was almost as good as the homes in the earthbag bible.

Esra turned from her perch, sponge in hand and wiped a splodge of mud from her face. 'Aw Ahmet, let's make a house like this. It's *lovely*!'

'You must be frigging joking!' shouted Ahmet as he powered the full wheelbarrow down the slope. 'I'm not making *nothing* without concrete.'

I jumped off the ledge and pulled off my rubber gloves. It was time to call it a day. Ahmet and Celal had generated a veritable dirt mountain and were now throwing some clay into it. Ahmet scooped a small hole in the centre of the mountain before dropping his shovel. He pulled over a large water canister and poured it into the central well. Celal pulled the edges of the plastic sheeting up and threw them over the top of the pile. A new Jabba the Hutt was in the making and he would sit stewing like that until the next work day.

The fatigue pulled at my bones. It dragged on my legs and my arms as though someone had turned up the gravity dial to mimic Jupiter. Staggering over to my tent, I watched the team dip their hands one by one into the water tank to scrub off the mud. I unzipped my tent and poked my head inside. Then I turned around and fell backwards. I let my head and shoulders rest on the carpet inside, my torso was on the wooden platform outside, and my legs and booted feet dangled from the edge. 'Let's take a rest tomorrow,' I groaned to the tent roof.

'Flipping Nora, I thought you'd never say it!' said Ahmet. Behind the tent, I heard the team tramp off to home.

Facade

Adnan left the next day. I watched him frantically packing a black rucksack with cameras and sound equipment. As he tottered down the tiled steps of his little white house on the hill, he handed me his keys.

'Use it as much as you like until your house is done. I'd prefer someone benefitted from the space while I'm not around,' he said. I gratefully slid the key ring into my pocket and followed him to the car. The sun had disappeared that day leaving the sky bereft and grey. I shivered as I opened the boot of my donkey-buzzard. Adnan threw his backpack in and heaved the lid shut with a bang.

'I'm pissed I never saw the house finished,' he said as he slid into the passenger seat.

'Ah, I'll send you some photos after Christmas,' I replied. I pumped the gas pedal to get the LPG flowing and started up the engine.

Negotiating cracks and bumps and sudden jolts, we silently motored over Yapraklı's swerving black road. It was like driving along the crusty back of an old dragon. As the mountains soared in front of us and the valley plunged away beside us, a cool steam rose from the crevices. The dragon might have been sleeping, but it was still puffing smoke.

I deposited Adnan at the bus stop on the main road. As he stood with his bags on the gravel, he ran a hand through his jet black hair. Then he held out his arms. I hugged him tight.

'What can I say, brother? Thank you for everything you've done.'

'Ah, it was an awesome adventure! I've just gotta get this next story done, then I'll be back,' he said and stooped to pick up his rucksack.

I climbed back into the car and waved. As I pulled away from the stop and trundled back over the snaking black vertebrae of the mountain road, it felt like the end of an era. Though it had not even lasted a couple of months, the earthbag voyage seemed to have reached some sort of terminus. Seemed. In truth, journeys never really begin or end. They are in constant motion, each destination leading to the next. Still, I only had days before my flight to the UK and a Christmas of copious alcohol and overeating. I wondered how far we could progress with the plaster before I left. As it turned out, the answer was, not very.

As the day forged on, the brow of the sky lowered in a thick, grey band. I walked to my land to study the house. Now that I was alone, everything looked different. With the exception of the small, front panel that Esra and I had smoothed, the rest appeared something of a botch up, as though my lovely little earthbag roundhouse had contracted an unsightly mud disease. Brown clumps besmirched the orange walls, and as they dried they became uglier. I suddenly suffered a relapse of perfectionism. I remembered the earthbag bible and the pictures of the aesthetic interiors, the cosy alcoves and the eye-catching sculptures. At present my mud finish was as far from those images of beauty as the cladding on a supermarket warehouse. I closed my eyes.

It was then the rain began to fall. It was hardly a downpour, more a sullen drizzle. I pulled up the hood of my macintosh. As I left my property and walked up the hill to Adnan's house, I calmed myself with the thought that the final earthplaster coat would hide all the blemishes. I'd just have to persevere until I forged the look I was yearning. The raindrops thickened a little as I reached Adnan's muddy driveway, the evergreens squirming as the watery beads hit their leaves. Turning the key in the lock, I opened the wooden door. Then I put the kettle on for a cup of tea.

As it happened, my hopes for plaster progress were scuppered. At the time I was frustrated. I just wanted to have that plaster on. But I should have paused to consider if perhaps the weather was doing me a favour.

The next day, as the rain spattered against the windows of Adnan's house, I pulled out the earthbag bible again. I turned the mud-smeared pages nostalgically, from the foundations through to the roof. Then I stared at the earthbag show houses with their immaculate facades. Some stood proudly under attractive raw mud finishes. Most

241

paraded under a smooth lime coat. They were dream homes. I closed the book, and pondered on the obsession, even in the natural building world, for the perfect house; an abode to show off to your neighbours, something to boast to your friends about. I was aware that one-upmanship was the unattractive lath coat lurking beneath my anxiety about the earthplaster. I was worrying about what others thought, especially as I'd spent the past six weeks telling them all to go and eat dirt.

Throwing the book onto the table, I looked out the window. The slope outside had turned into a bubbling white river as a flock of sheep poured down the bank, braying and chewing as they went. They nibbled happily on grass stalks and bushes, jostling with their neighbours and nosing their bouncing kids. In fact, if you watch sheep, that's all they do, day after day; wander about the mountains with their friends and family, eating. When night comes they snuggle up in a cosy barn. It's not a bad life, better than that of quite a few humans. I wondered why we *Homo sapiens* had made ours so untenably complicated, with our fragile egos, our incurable status anxiety and our desperate need to feel important or respected. Where did we lose the sense of our innate worth?

I moved my gaze from outside to inside, somewhere crossing a point of exchange. Like the sheep, I was wandering the hills of life, hunkering down here and there in the barn of the moment. My home had at various times been a city flat, a five star hotel room, a grotty windowless guesthouse, a seaside bamboo hut, a village house, a tent on a mountain. Right now it was Adnan's house. In a day or two it would be a bedroom in Essex. This is what a home essentially is; a temporary shelter, nothing more. The rest of it, the cladding, the paint and the wallpaper, the new furniture, the decking, the ornaments, the pictures, the Artex, the curtain rails, the brass taps, the antique rugs, the polished floorboards, the state of the art salt and pepper grinders, are nothing but our attempts to inscribe ourselves onto our surroundings, to prove to 'out there' how important 'in here' really is. To hide the truth that 'in here' is basically empty.

The whitewashed wall of Adnan's house was littered with hairline cracks. They ran through the plaster in tiny lightning forks. I stood up. Then I reached for my rucksack and began filling it with my dirty washing. The rain kept coming down.

***

Two days later, I was far from the sheep and the mountains and the earthbag house. I was in Essex snuggled under a duvet in my dad's house contemplating the wonders of the modern world. There were taps with water gushing out, heat at the touch of a button, washing machines, kettles, piping hot power showers, drinks cabinets and boxes of Quality

Street. I slept for hours, showered twice a day and even vegetated in front of the television. It was as though I'd boarded a trans-galactic shuttle from The Mud and now found myself on Planet Modernity.

As I expounded my exploits to my family and friends, I watched faces crumple in horror or drift off in boredom. No matter how hard I tried to explain the excitement and wonder of my adventure, I couldn't communicate it. People blinked or winced, then pressed the remote control. There are few dangers in the modern world, any creases of risk ironed out by health and safety. There is little dirt and even less discomfort. Convenience is King and gratification is his whore. I wouldn't deny, after six months of rough living on a hill, where even grabbing a shower or taking a pee was an energetic outdoor pursuit, I was tired, and King Convenience gave me a break. Yet up to what point?

Once the grime has been washed off and the muscles have recuperated, a dull veneer begins to coat the life of us moderns. The insidious padded cell of the comfort zone encircles us. And when it does, something precious is lost. Without danger, where is the courage? Without dirt, where is passion? Without allowing discomfort, how does one truly connect? For there is a happiness that stretches far deeper and wider than the short-lived superficial stabs of pleasure gratification can offer. There is a profound joy that underpins the natural life, and a magic that over-arcs it. The deepest meaning skulks in tiny details and beauty unfolds at every turn. How can one feel bored when nature's picture is never still, never once the same as it was five minutes before? Unconsciously the modern world mourns the loss of its natural essence. Suffering bouts of psychic dissatisfaction, its inhabitants are left with nothing to fill the gap other than anti-depressants, alcohol, and Facebook.

Before long I missed the feel of the dirt. I thought of the slapdash mud walls of my home and stuck my bottom lip out. *Pah!* I said to myself. *Who cares? I'm moving in as soon as I get back.*

Cracks

It was mid-January. A new year with a new mission. I drove from the airport and along the rocky hem of the Bey Mountains that tower the length of Turkey's turquoise coast. Eventually, the highway thinned and the traffic lights disappeared. Mount Olympos rose from the pine forests like the home of the gods it is. Its peak was now capped with a crown of white snow. Winter had arrived. I contemplated moving in to my house and banged the steering wheel in excitement. I couldn't wait.

It was a little after midday when I rumbled down the russet dirt track to my property. As the car veered the first corner, I gasped at the view. A deep, green gown of pristine forest swept the length of the mountain slopes, culminating at the sea. The valley was a goddess and she was dressed to kill.

I parked just above my land and unloaded my bags from the car. Then I picked my way through the squelching mud, past the lime bag obelisk at the entrance, past the compost heap and round the corner. The house loomed before me. On seeing the plaster, my heart nearly stopped beating. Everywhere enormous cracks zigzagged along the mud walls. It looked like a circular Arizona.

Dropping the bags, I ran up to the walls and walked around them. The cracks were great gashes. In places the plaster had simply fallen off. It was so ugly and demonstrably unsound, the house would clearly have to be entirely re-plastered. That would take weeks. Meanwhile I was clean out of money.

I hadn't thought about money for a while. I'd deftly swept it under the rugs of my grey matter, hoping the issue would drop through the gaps in reality's floorboards and out of sight. This was a witless approach to a serious problem. In fact, I had little over $1000 left in my account and hadn't even considered the prospect of earning more.

I slumped on a rock and stared glumly at what should have been my new world, but wasn't. I wondered what to do. Shivering in the cold winter air, I pulled out my phone and called the long-suffering Chris. The sky blanched above me. A branch from the olive tree in front of me bowed in the wind. The phone picked up. How wretched I felt as I relayed the state of my plaster. I was very much on the brink of tears.

'Ah don't be disappointed,' he said. 'It's all part of the creation process. You'll find a solution.'

That moment is a poignant one for me. The moment of sitting on the rock and hearing my disappointment echoed back at me. Because I *was* inordinately disappointed. In my mind's eye, it was as if the plaster cracks had destroyed my entire house. My vision was ruined. My plan was wrecked. And yes, despite all my crowing about not planning, inadvertently, I *had* harboured a scheme, albeit harebrained and haphazard. The plan was to move into my house and live on next to nothing for a while until I gathered enough strength to create another plan to save me financially. It wasn't much of a strategy, the forward thinking equivalent of Tarzan swinging through life's jungle on lianas. The last vine had just slipped out of my grasp.

That night, in a bid to stay warm, I slept at a friend's house in the valley. I was now feeling very much the refugee wandering from neighbour to neighbour in an effort to escape the cold and the wet. I could have used Adnan's house, and sometimes did, but he had other guests coming and going, and I was tired of making new friends. I tended to move in when it was empty and out again when it filled up. I wasn't about to give up though. Against all reason, I pitted myself against the truth, that I just didn't have the funds. I called Celal to come and sort the plaster out the very next day.

'Hmph. Shoulda put lime in, told yer so,' Celal muttered as he wandered round the circle tapping the mud panels and pulling bits of plaster off here and there. It reminded me of a beautician ripping off depilatory wax. Every time he yanked off a chunk, I winced. Soon, he wandered over to the east side of the house, to where his experimental lime batches had been applied. I trailed him like one of his menagerie of animals, bottom lip protruding. Halting at the appropriate spot, we studied the wall. Celal's two pale patches of plaster stood out from the rest, a) because they were lighter in colour, and b) because they were noticeably smoother, and devoid of cracks.

'See. Lime. You need lime.'

I did see. 'I think we need more straw too. The straw is binding it somehow,' I added.

So we returned to the drawing board. As the sun moved up the sky, we huddled about our small remaining hillock of mud/clay mixture. Rolling up our sleeves and pulling on our rubber gloves, we hunched over the cauldron of the wheelbarrow with yoghurt pots of mud, straw and lime – a couple of muck alchemists forging a new element. We stirred and pummelled and squeezed the sludge until we had obtained the look we thought we wanted. By midday we had cooked up three new batches; one with more lime in, one with more straw in and a final wildcard concoction with only straw and lime.

'We'll need to leave 'em a week to see what happens.' Celal was troweling our experimental straw and lime mix onto the inside wall. I frowned at it. Without the mud it didn't seem to have much consistency.

'Pff, what are we supposed to do while we wait for it to dry?'

'Dunno. Go on holiday?' Celal grinned.

'And this afternoon?'

'Let's take a look at that floor. You any idea how we're gonna make the boards go round? Like what we gonna bang 'em on to?'

I leaned against the wall. Another chunk of plaster was dislodged. It wobbled in its socket like a rotten tooth. I thought for a moment. The floor joists. Yes. Somehow we were going to have to cut a pack of 5-by-10s and fix them round the edge of the floor to create a circle. It was the kind of fiddly job I hated.

That afternoon, with the sun creeping tentatively through the clouds, Celal and I abandoned the mud plaster to its fate and set about the floor. We measured and sawed beams, but it was a devil of a job to hack them to the right angle so they'd fit between the joists. We experienced even more trouble nailing them level. The process seemed to be taking forever, and the result was highly unsatisfactory in that because the walls were round and the joists straight, there was always a gap left which meant the ends of floorboards, when nailed down, were flapping in mid-air. By evening I had a headache from concentrating.

'This isn't working, Celal.'

'Aye, thass the trouble with a round house. It woulda been a lot easier if you'd made it square.'

Thanks for stating the obvious I roared inside my head and threw the hammer on the floor in disgust. Celal blinked. Then he began collecting up the stray nails. We both climbed out of the house, and walked along the path from my land, Celal to his home, me to Adnan's house. As we trudged up the slope together, I computed that somehow we needed to make the wood curve. But how?

Time and Money

Adnan's house was a cheerless icebox now that he was gone and I was alone. I did my best to mitigate the desolation by stuffing the stove to the brim with firewood and brewing some tea on it. I perched at the table listening to the pot wheeze and pulled my laptop toward me. Inserting the dongle, I waited for it to connect to the internet. Then I took a deep breath, logged into my bank account and prepared for the worst.

Whichever way I looked at it, and however many currency conversions I made, about $1250 remained. I was stumped. The mud plaster test batches needed a week to dry. I was still short of windows and doors which would bite greedily into my shrunken money pie. I had at least two more months of winter before I could feasibly move back into my tent. Either I had to stop spending money, or I had to earn some. After so much hope, determination and effort, this harsh fact was dispiriting. So I did what so many of us do when life looks like a leaky barrel of effluent and we'd like to forget about it, I logged into Facebook.

In a semi-conscious haze, I scrolled down the newsfeed blankly ingesting the photos of cats smoking cigars, the bossy memes telling me life was what I made it, and the baffling status updates along the lines of 'Don't you just hate it when your co-worker steals a paperclip and *doesn't* replace it'. Somewhere, while wading across this social media marshland, I became aware of friends in Taiwan referring to their holiday plans for Chinese New Year. The cogs in my head clicked slowly into motion. Chinese New Year is *the* prime time to procure a last minute teaching job in Taiwan, because there's always someone, who having wriggled out of the clutches of the educational leviathan and run for their life to Thailand, has left an urgent vacancy in their wake. I started reminiscing on the joys of tofu and *dan bing*, a Taiwanese breakfast pancake I'm partial to. I imagined sleeping for more than a week in the same room, a room which came with a hot shower and a bed, a room I could legitimately call my own. My $1250 was just about enough to fly me to Taipei and start me up – if I had a job set up before I went. The only question was, could I possibly survive another round of teaching?

Opening up my email, I flicked through my list of contacts until I found the supervisor of my former school. I threw the universe a gauntlet. I would only accept a job if I was offered a six month contract and a pay rise. Obtaining a contract for less than a year in the teaching world, especially in Taiwan, is nigh on impossible. I don't think I know anyone else who's managed it. To ask for a pay rise on top, as well as your end of contract bonus, is supremely cheeky. Yet, I couldn't endure more than six months, and I needed to make it financially worth my while. Throwing my destiny to providence, I typed the mail, pressed the send button and then shut down my computer.

The very next day I received a reply. As I clicked on the mail, I gulped. The answer was yes to all my conditions. I hadn't expected such a sudden and positive response. Now, I had some *serious* decision making to do. Was I really going to go through with this? What would I do with my car? What about the plaster on the house? Where would I put my stuff? As I was contemplating all the above, the windows rattled. I glanced out of the window and gulped a second time. The sky was as black as the soul of Hades, the granite clouds belting overhead, a nebular war battalion about to invade. I stood up and opened the door. My hair was immediately whipped into my eyes. Outside was churning in agitation. Leaves spun in brown vortexes, treetops bent and buckled, and the wind whistled as it drove through the barns and round the house. The long-awaited Mediterranean winter storm was imminent.

Shoving the door to, I scurried into the bedroom and located my keys. Then I donned my macintosh and wellington boots. Bracing myself for a gale force suction wind, I opened the front door again and battled to keep it on its hinges. Head down, I pushed outside, slammed the door and made for my car. If I didn't move the donkey-buzzard up to the main road, it would be stranded in the mud of Adnan's track for days. Fat blobs of rain began to plop to the ground, the drops breaking on the steps like soft, wet fruit. I reached the car and started her up. Then I roared up Adnan's muddy drive and parked on the tarmac at the top.

As I opened the car door, I hung onto it for dear life. The rain was no longer plopping but driving down. Slamming the door closed, I fumbled for the key to lock it. By the time I put the key back in my pocket, I could feel the macintosh sticking to my arms. Ignoring the longer but smoother road back to the house, I cantered down a thistle covered slope feeling the rain already coursing down the front of my coat. When I reached the front door again, I was writhing in the discomfort of soggy underwear. The house was now dark. I reached for the light switch. It was no surprise to find the power off.

The storm rolled and raved for two days. I stayed in Adnan's house one night before driving to the nearest metropolis of Antalya for a cappuccino and a chat with friends. After so long in the mud-laden folds of nature, the city was a concrete contrivance. The incessant whirr of the cars, the stink of polluted air and the sheer misery crawling over the majority of faces was sobering. Nonetheless, there were some things the city could do better than the country; good coffee and cakes were two of them.

Sitting in a warm, dry café overlooking the mountainous bay of Antalya, I stuck a wedge of tiramisu in my mouth and sighed in satisfaction.

'I'd do it. Just go. Get yourself back on track. And it might be great to have a change, eh?' said one of my

American friends. She looked longingly at my dessert, and raised her hand to the waiter, 'Hey, can I have one of those?'

'But what about the house? And the car?' I leaned back in my chair and closed my eyes.

'Ah these are all just practicalities. They can be taken care of. The car can stay at mine for six months. You can cover the house in a tarp or something.' She stirred a large mug containing one of those sugary, cream-decorated cocktails Americans refer to as coffee.

I stared out at the sea. It looked like a dark meringue, white-capped waves rising over the surface as the wind mercilessly beat the water. I sighed. It was an exhalation that seemed to originate from a place infinitely deeper than my lungs.

***

The next day, with half of the past two days downpour now careering through Antalya's creaking drainage system (the other half filled the roads in a Turkish parody of Venice), I drove back to my land. After the storm, my own road had become unusable. Great gulches of mud weaved through the track like thick, brown anacondas, and in places the track had been ripped apart. Where the rain had coursed down the slope, it had carved chasms out of the dirt leaving nothing but boulders jutting up like fangs. I parked my donkey-buzzard at the top by the graveyard where I ferried my water from, put on my wellington boots and walked the 800 metres down to my house.

The sky was still frothy, and a fresh wind gushed through the trees. My cheeks smarted and my eyes watered from the rushing air. Rucksack bouncing, I squelched to the bottom of the incline, turned past the compost heap and the wall of hydraulic lime, and down to my tent platform. I stopped. Then I clapped a hand over my mouth. Oh dear.

My poor old Carrefour tent was hanging from the wooden posts, broken limbs of the tent poles jutting out of the canvas at odd angles. It was a torn and battered skin. As I examined closer, I saw my mattress and some of my bed sheets scattered over the slope. The tent had regurgitated the *kilim* from the front door, and it lolled there, wet and coiled like a huge green tongue. Days later I'd find pillows in obscure corners of the forest.

Further inspection revealed that my kitchen had become a rain collecting bog, and the bathroom had all but disappeared – mirror in broken pieces on the floor, white towel hanging on a branch – a fluffy, mud-splashed flag of surrender. My home was wrecked. Climbing back to the top of the land, I sat on the edge of my wooden platform and patted the tent affectionately. Then I laughed. If this wasn't a kick out, I don't know what was. Certainly one needs determination to build a home, one needs staying power to forge on to the end. But at some point, one has to know when to quit. Finally I accepted the truth. It was over. For now.

I walked to my earthbag house. I was so near to having a proper home, and yet simultaneously so far. The exoskeleton of the house was solid and dry. The round roof with its bamboo ceiling looked fantastic. But the windows were tapering peculiarities. The floor was a plastic-covered rectangular island with gaps all around, and the plaster? It didn't bear looking at.

Taking a stool from behind the shed, I placed it in the centre of my earthbag house and parked myself on it with my rucksack by my feet. I looked through the doorway out onto the valley. The pomegranate trees now stood bare. The hills were saturated, the roads brown sloughs. I could feel it; the sleepiness in the mist spreading through the vale. Winter was Gaia's bedtime, time to hibernate, to rest and recover ready for the next year's adventure.

'Ah fuck it!' I whispered to the thick mud walls. Reaching down to my rucksack, I pulled out my laptop and dongle. I turned it on and waited for the screen to dance. It took me about twenty minutes to book a flight to Taipei. I was leaving in less than ten days.

Epilogue

Six months later I would return to my little mud home on the hill. I would gather the earthbag team once more and doggedly persevere with the earthplaster, throwing mud ball after mud ball at the walls. It only took me another year. Eventually, the doors and windows would be miraculously straightened, and the floor would curve as well. Ultimately, it became the beautiful little roundhouse of my dreams. One thing I would never do though, is teach again. The juxtaposition of a life of ultimate freedom in nature's bosom and a life of ordered comfort as a wage slave made it clear to me. You see, I hadn't just been building a home. I'd been building a life. I'd created an entirely new world in which I was the sovereign, where bosses and governments, economies and debt, the patriarch and social pressure had little or no power. I decided to try and eradicate the need for money in my world. I aimed to be power independent, water independent and money independent. Becoming the second person in Turkey to successfully complete an earthbag house, something I'd had no training for and no experience of, made me realise that if I wanted I could probably do *anything*. And this is true. We can, if we want, do anything. There's only one thing stopping any of us. The often silent but pernicious 'You'll *never* be able to do this' rumbling around the backrooms of our heads.

Once one has tasted true freedom, who would willingly give it up? Once one experiences the moment to moment beauty of the natural world, what interest is an iPhone? On sensing the magic oozing out of this cosmic orb of mud we call Earth, how can one agree to spend all day in an office? When I returned from my six month slog in Taiwan, I vowed to eat the grass before I flogged my soul to the machine ever again. Later, as the money I'd earned in the system dwindled, I was tested to the wire on that one. But that, as they say, is another story.

www.themudhome.com

www.themudhome.com

If you enjoyed Mud Ball, please leave a review with the online distributor of your choice, or with Goodreads. It will be greatly appreciated.

***

Atulya K Bingham also wrote the novel *Ayşe's Trail* which won the One Big Book Launch in 2014. She lives in her earthbag house in the Turkish hills with her absurdly sociable dog Rotty, Grandmother Olive, a large vegetable garden, owls, agama lizards, squirrels, snakes, scorpions, camel spiders, two toads (one in the kitchen, one under the gazebo), a robin, and a magpie. Apo pops by regularly to say hello, too. The earthbag team, for the most part remain in the area with the exception of Celal who sadly passed away in 2014.

You can follow Atulya K Bingham's comings and goings about The Mud from her blog and website: www.themudhome.com

Travelogue meets historical fiction along Turkey's Lycian Way.

Ayşe's Trail was selected for Completely Novel's One Big Book Launch in the UK 2014.

Ayşe, a 38-year-old mother from Istanbul, decides to tackle the Lycian Way in southern Turkey. She has never camped alone before. As she strikes out into Lycia's ancient forests, she is on a quest to leave behind the past and find her own truth. But the Lycian Way is steeped in memories. Unknown to Ayşe, she is walking in someone else's footsteps. 2500 years earlier, when Lycia was an independent state and worshipped the Goddess Leto, the Persian general Harpagos was stomping along the very same road in a bid to take over the ancient world.

Read more about Ayşe's Trail from www.atulyakbingham.com

CPSIA information can be obtained at www.ICGtesting.com
Printed in the USA
BVOW06s2219170116

433212BV00002B/86/P